Prayers
for Hard Times

Reflections, Meditations, and
Inspirations of Hope and Comfort

Becca Anderson

Cover Design: Elina Diaz
Layout & Design: Roberto Nunez

For permission requests, please contact the publisher at:
Mango Publishing Group
2850 Douglas Road, 3rd Floor
Coral Gables, FL 33134 USA
info@mango.bz

For special orders, quantity sales, course adoptions and corporate sales, please email the publisher at sales@mango.bz. For trade and wholesale sales, please contact Ingram Publisher Services at customer.service@ingramcontent.com or +1.800.509.4887.

Prayers for Hard Times: Reflections, Meditations and Inspirations of Hope and Comfort

Library of Congress Cataloging-in-Publication number: 2017960351
ISBN: (paperback) 978-1-63353-529-9, (ebook) 978-1-63353-653-1
BISAC category code: REL036000 RELIGION / Inspirational

Printed in the United States of America

Table of Contents

Introduction

Let Not Your Heart Be Troubled

Dear Reader,

The paths of our lives take many twists and turns and just as
many ups and downs. I firmly agree with those who say you can't
recognize the good times if you haven't experienced the opposite.
I also believe that going through difficulties builds character and
makes us more resilient. But why, oh why do the tough times have
to be so hard? I had the idea for this book ten years ago when a
loved one, my fiancé, was diagnosed with stage IV cancer with very
few options. I was his primary caretaker, and I did my best to paste
on a smile, speak about a positive future, and above all, stay upbeat
for him. He was unable to work, so I was also the breadwinner; I
arranged a steady stream of meal deliveries and friendly visitors
while I worked my very long days. One day I was at a business
lunch with an author who asked me how I was handling this.
Suddenly, I was gasping for breath and had to run outside. I had
to go home; after a couple more episodes, I went to the emergency
room. I was diagnosed with stress-induced asthma and prescribed
heavy-duty medications and ordered to rest. But I knew I couldn't
sleep this off. The medications took effect after a couple of days,
but the feeling that I was being suffocated by stress did not
dissipate at all. To add to the load, I felt like I needed to be strong

for someone else and that I was going to fail him. He passed very quickly, which somehow compounded the grief. We had barely had time to adjust to the severity of his illness when he died. One of the blessings to come from this was that his family and friends became a very close-knit group and have remained so, sharing memories and making new ones.

When the vicissitudes of life remind me that the only constant is change, I think back to those dark days and reflect on how it felt, oftentimes hopeless with a depthless sadness. The only thing that helped me was praying and reading the wisdom of others. I remembered wishing I had a book that I could carry with me at all times just so I could turn to it when I felt I just could not go on. I know you, dear reader, have also faced circumstances that seemed insurmountable. My sincere hope is that the prayers and homilies I have gathered here offer some comfort and courage to you. I would love to hear from you—tell me the stories of what you and your loved ones have lived through and overcome. I would love to hear your encouraging words and gain strength from you.

With gratitude and blessings,
Becca Anderson

When Everything is New Again

"Fall seven times, stand up eight."
—Japanese proverb

"Sometimes our light goes out, but is blown again into instant flame by an encounter with another human being."
—Albert Schweitzer

"We should always pray for help, but we should always listen for inspiration and impression to proceed in ways different from those we may have thought of."
—John H. Groberg

"A problem is a chance for you to do your best."
—Duke Ellington

The Fearsome Blessing of Hard Times

The fearsome blessing of that hard time continues to work itself out in my life in the same way we're told the universe is still hurtling through outer space under impact of the great cosmic explosion that brought it into being in the first place. I think grace sometimes explodes into our lives like that—sending out pain, terror, astonishment through inner space until by grace they become Orion, Cassiopeia, Polaris, to give us our bearings, to bring us into something like full being at last.

- Frederick Buechner

You Will Have Peace

The Lord bless you and keep you;
The Lord make his face shine upon you and be gracious to you;
The Lord turn his face toward you and give you peace.

—Numbers 6:24–26, The Bible, NIV

By the Awful Grace of God

And even in our sleep,
pain that cannot forget
falls drop by drop upon the heart,
and in our own despite,
against our will,

comes wisdom to us
by the awful grace of God.

—*Agamemnon, Aeschylus – 5th Century BC*

Calling All Angels

Angel of God,
my guardian dear,
to whom God's love commits me here,
ever this day,
be at my side
to light and guard,
to rule and guide.

- Catholic Liturgy—A Prayer to Guardian Angels

Inspire Me to Kindness, Each and Every Day

Day by day,
Let me see the grace
Day by day,
Let me see the way

Day by day,
Let me see the beauty
Let me hear the music

day by day
Let me see the way

Day by day
let me see the goodness
Let me feel the love
Inspire me to kindness
Day by day,
let me see the way

Let me see the grace
Let me see the way

- Day by Day—Hans van Rostenberghe

Growing Old

I am of the nature to grow old.
There is no way to escape growing old.

I am of the nature to have ill-health.
There is no way to escape having ill-health.

I am of the nature to die.
There is no way to escape death.

All that is dear to me and everyone I love
are of the nature to change.
There is no way to escape being separated from them.

My actions are my only true belongings.
I cannot escape the consequences of my actions.
My actions are the ground on which I stand.

- Buddha

Give Us the Power To Heal

Hail to thee, day! Hail, ye day's sons!
Hail, night and daughter of night!
With blithe eyes look on both of us:
send to those sitting here speed!

Hail to you, Gods! Hail, Goddesses!
Hail, earth that gives to all!
Goodly spells and speech bespeak we from you,
and healing hands, in this life.

- The Poetic Edda—the Lay of Sigrdrifa, 600 AD

Prayer to St. Joseph the Protector

O St. Joseph whose protection is so great, so strong,
so prompt before the Throne of God,
I place in you all my interests and desires.
O St. Joseph do assist me by your powerful intercession
and obtain for me from your Divine Son
all spiritual blessings through Jesus Christ, Our Lord;
so that having engaged here below your Heavenly power

I may offer my Thanksgiving and Homage
to the most Loving of Fathers.
O St. Joseph, I never weary contemplating you
and Jesus asleep in your arms.
I dare not approach while He reposes near your heart.
Press him in my name and kiss His fine Head for me,
and ask Him to return the Kiss when I draw my dying breath.
St. Joseph, Patron of departing souls,
pray for us.
Amen..

- Prayer to St. Joseph, Patron of the Dying, 100 AD

Celtic Prayer for Protection

Give thou thine heart to the wild magic,
To the Lord and the Lady of Nature,
Beyond any consideration of this world.

Do not covet large or small,
Do not despise weakling or poor,
Semblance of evil allow not near thee,
Never give nor earn thou shame.

The Ancient Harmonies are given thee,
Understand them early and prove,
Be one with the power of the elements,
Put behind thee dishonor and lies.

Be loyal to the Lord of the Wild Wood,
Be true to the Lady of the Stars,
Be true to thine own self besides,
True to the magic of Nature above all else.

Do not thou curse anyone,
Lest thou threefold cursed shouldst be,
And shouldst thou travel ocean and earth,
Follow the very step of the ancient trackways.

- Celtic Oral Tradition, 800 AD

A Prayer for All Prisoners

Abba Father, Loving God, our hope and our salvation

—Calm us –
Give us the assurance of your presence

—Empty us –
Make us pure vessels of your love

—Polish us –
Shine each of us to be a reflection of your grace

—Equip us –
Arm all of us, Father, to be your strong warriors.

Right now, today,
We are yours and we are thankful.

Amen..

- C. Lee Davis of the Prison Ministry

Fare Thee Well

May the road rise up to meet you.
May the wind be always at your back.
May the sun shine warm upon your face,
the rains fall soft upon your fields,

and until we meet again,
may God hold you in the palm of His hand.

- Irish Blessing

Prayer for Acceptance

O! Thou God of all beings, of all worlds, and of all times,
We pray that the little differences in our clothes,
in our inadequate languages,
in our ridiculous customs,
in our imperfect laws,
in our illogical opinions,
in our ranks and conditions which
are so disproportionately important to us
and so meaningless to you,
that these small variations
that distinguish those atoms that we call men,

one from another,
may not be signals of hatred and persecution!

- Voltaire, 1756

With a Strong Heart and a Cheerful Will

Almighty Father
whose way is in the sea
and whose paths are in the great waters
whose command is over all and whose love never faileth:
Let me be aware of Thy presence
and obedient to Thy will.
Keep me true to my best self
guarding me against dishonesty in purpose and in deed,
and helping me so to live
that I can stand unashamed and unafraid before my shipmates,
my loved ones, and Thee.

Protect those in whose love I live.
Give me the will to do the work of a man
and to accept my share of responsibilities
with a strong heart and a cheerful mind.
Make me considerate of those entrusted to my leadership and
faithful to the duties my country has entrusted to me.
Let my uniform remind me daily
of the traditions of the Service of which I am a part.

If I am inclined to doubt, steady my faith;
if I am tempted, make me strong to resist;

---

if I should miss the mark, give me courage to try again.
Guide me with the light of truth, and keep before me the life of
Him
by whose example and help I trust
to obtain the answer to my prayer,
Jesus Christ, our Lord.

Amen..

- World War II - Naval Serviceman

What Doesn't Kill You Makes You Stronger

God does not send us despair in order to kill us; he
sends it in order to awaken us to new life.

- Reflections - Hermann Hesse

Start Your Day With Thankfulness

When you arise in the morning,
give thanks for the morning light,
for your life and strength.

Give thanks for your food, and the joy of living.

If you see no reason for giving thanks, the fault lies with yourself.

- Tecumseh, Shawnee Chief

Prayer to Start Every Day

Don't worry,
be happy!

- Meher Baba, 1966

As You and I Are One

Father, may they all be one,
as you and I are one.

- John 17:11—The Final Prayer of Jesus

Prayer for Serenity

God, grant me
Serenity to accept the things I cannot change,
Courage to change the things I can,
and wisdom to know the difference.
Living one day at a time;
enjoying one moment at a time;
accepting hardship
as the pathway to peace.
Taking, as He did, this sinful world
as it is, not as I would have it;
trusting that He will make all things right
if I surrender to His will;

that I may be reasonably happy in this life
and supremely happy with Him forever in the next.

Amen..

- Reinhold Niebuhr

Prayer for Health and Happiness

Om sarvetra sukhinah santu sarve santu niramayah.
Sarve bhadrani pasyantu ma kascid duhkhamapnuyat
Om shantih shantih shantih

Oh Almighty! May everybody be happy!
May all be free from ailments!
May we see what is auspicious!
May no one be subject to miseries!
Oh Almighty! May there be a Peace! Peace! Peace! Everywhere.

- The Rig-Veda, India, 3700 BC

Reverence for All Life

From childhood, I felt a compassion for animals. Even before I
started
school, I found it impossible to understand why, in my evening
prayers,
I should pray only for human beings. Consequently, after my
mother

had prayed with me and had given me a good-night kiss, I secretly recited another prayer, one I had composed myself. It went like this:

Dear God, protect and bless all living beings.
Keep them from evil and let them sleep in peace.

- Dr. Albert Schweitzer, 1964

My Religion Is Kindness

If you wish to experience peace, provide peace for another.
If you wish to know that you are safe, cause another to know that they are safe.
If you wish to better understand seemingly incomprehensible things,
help another to better understand.
If you wish to heal your own sadness or anger, seek to heal the sadness or anger of another.
Those others are waiting for you now. They are looking to you for guidance,
for help, for courage, for strength, for understanding, and for assurance at this hour.
Most of all, they are looking to you for love.
My religion is very simple.
My religion is kindness.

- His Holiness the 14th Dalai Lama, 1981

Remain in the Light of Love

God, help me to be
a pure vehicle for your love
and light
and wisdom.

- Steven Sadleir

We Are All the Children of God

Blessed are the poor in spirit:
for theirs is the kingdom of heaven.

Blessed are they that mourn:
for they shall be comforted.

Blessed are the meek:
for they shall inherit the earth.

Blessed are they which do hunger and thirst after righteousness:
for they shall be filled.

Blessed are the merciful:
for they shall obtain mercy.

Blessed are the pure in heart:
for they shall see God.

Blessed are the peacemakers:

for they will be called the children of God.

- The Beatitudes, Matthew 5:3-9

Believe More Deeply

Believe more deeply.
Hold your face up to the light,
even though for the moment you do not see.

- Bill Wilson, Cofounder of Alcoholics Anonymous

Rest in the Arms of Loving Providence

My God, I am yours for time and eternity.
Teach me to cast myself entirely
into the arms of your loving Providence
with a lively, unlimited confidence in your compassionate, tender
pity.
Grant, O most merciful Redeemer,
That whatever you ordain or permit may be acceptable to me.
Take from my heart all painful anxiety;
let nothing sadden me but sin,
nothing delight me but the hope
of coming to the possession of You,
my God and my all,

in your everlasting kingdom.
Amen..

- Suscipe of Catherine McAuley - 1778–1841

Loving Your Enemies

Oh God, help us in our lives and in all of our attitudes,
to work out this controlling force of love,
this controlling power that can solve
every problem that we confront in all areas.
Oh, we talk about politics;
we talk about the problems facing our atomic civilization.
Grant that all men will come together and discover
that as we solve the crisis and solve these problems,
the international problems,
the problems of atomic energy,
the problems of nuclear energy,
and yes, even the race problem;
let us join together in a great fellowship of love
and bow down at the feet of Jesus.
Give us this strong determination.
In the name and spirit of this Christ, we pray.
Amen..

- Dr. Martin Luther King, Jr.

Pray to the Heavens Above

God exists.

His place is very cool.
Look at how it is where God is.

- *Mesoamerican Indian Blessing*

The Good Road and the Road of Difficulties

Hey-a-a-hey! Hey-a-a-hey! Hey-a-a-hey! Hey-a-a-hey!

Grandfather, Great Spirit, once more behold me on earth
and lean to hear my feeble voice.
You lived first, and you are older than all need, older than all
prayer.
All things belong to you—the two-leggeds,
the four-leggeds, the wings of the air
and all green things that live.
You have set the powers of the four quarters
to cross each other.
The good road and road of difficulties
you have made to cross;
and where they cross, the place is holy.
Day in and day out, forever, you are the life of things.

Therefore I am sending a voice, Great Spirit,
my Grandfather, forgetting nothing you have made, the stars of the

universe
and the grasses of the earth.

You have said to me,
when I was still young and could hope,
that in difficulty I should send a voice four times,
once for each quarter of the earth,
and you would hear me.

Today I send a voice for a people in despair.

You have given me a sacred pipe,
and through this I should make my offering.
You see it now.

From the west, you have given me the cup
of living water and the sacred bow, the power to make life and to
destroy.
You have given me a sacred wind and the herb
from where the white giant lives –
the cleansing power and the healing.
The daybreak star and the pipe,
you have given from the east;
and from the south, the nation's sacred hoop
and the tree that was to bloom.
To the center of the world you have taken me
and showed the goodness and the beauty
and the strangeness of the greening earth, the only mother –
and there the spirit shapes of things,
as they should be,
you have shown to me and I have seen.

At the center of this sacred hoop you have said
that I should make the tree to bloom.

With tears running, O Great Spirit, Great Spirit, my Grandfather -
with running tears I must say now that
the tree has never bloomed.
A pitiful old man, you see me here,
and I have fallen away and have done nothing.
Here at the center of the world,
where you took me when I was young and taught me;
here, old, I stand, and the tree is withered,
Grandfather, my Grandfather!

Again, and maybe the last time on this earth,
I recall the great vision you sent me.
It may be that some little root of the sacred tree still lives.
Nourish it then, that it may leaf and bloom
and fill with singing birds.
Hear me, not for myself, but for my people; I am old.

Hear me that they may once more go back into the sacred hoop
and find the good red road, the shielding tree!

In sorrow I am sending a feeble voice,
O Six Powers of the World.
Hear me in my sorrow, for I may never call again.
O make my people live!

- Black Elk, 1930

Give Us This Day

Which art in heaven,
Hallowed be
Your holy name.
Thy Kingdom come,
Just let your will be done
On earth,
As it is in heaven.
Give us this day
Our daily bread.
Forgive us our debts,
As we forgive our debtors.
And lead us not
Into all temptation,
But deliver us He said,
I am Safe
Safe
I am Safe
Safe
Safe
Safe
Safe
Safe
Hallelujah
Hallelujah
Hallelujah

Hallelujah
I'm safe.

- Ruth Baxter, with passage adapted from Luke 11:2-4

May We Always Be Ready for the Long Journey

O, our Father the Sky, hear us
and make us strong.
O, our Mother the Earth, hear us
and give us support.
O Spirit of the East,
send us your Wisdom.
O Spirit of the South,
may we tread your path.
O Spirit of the West,
may we always be ready for the long journey.
O Spirit of the North, purify us
with your cleansing winds.

- Oglala Sioux Tribal Chant

Be With Us and Hear Us

Fire of the Spirit
Life of the lives of creatures
Spiral of sanctity

Bond of all natures
Glow of charity
Lights of clarity
Taste of sweetness to the fallen
Be with us and hear us.

- Hildegarde of Bingen, 1169 AD

The Season of the Heart

"Just as despair can come to one only from other human beings, hope, too, can be given to one only by other human beings."
—Elie Wiesel

"The greatest glory in living lies not in never failing, but in rising every time we fail."
—Nelson Mandela

"In times of great stress or adversity, it's always best to keep busy, to plow your energy into something positive."
—Lee Iacocca

"It is only in our darkest hours that we may discover the true strength of the brilliant light within ourselves that can never, ever, be dimmed."
—Doe Zantamata

The Buddha's Guide to Gratitude

Give thanks

For what has been given to you,

However little.

Be pure, never falter.

- Buddha

There Is Enough for Everybody

May all be fed.

May all be healed.

May all be loved.

- John Robbins, 2002

Kind Regards

Forgive us every face we cannot look upon with joy.

- Frederick Buechner

God's Shield to Protect Me

I arise today through a mighty strength,
the invocation of the Trinity, through belief in the Threeness,
through confession of the Oneness of the Creator of creation.

I arise today through the strength of Christ with his Baptism,
through the strength of His Crucifixion with His Burial,
through the strength of His Resurrection with His Ascension,
through the strength of His descent for the Judgment of Doom.

I arise today through the strength of the love of Cherubim
in obedience of Angels, in the service of the Archangels,
in hope of resurrection to meet with reward,
in prayers of Patriarchs, in predictions of Prophets,
in preachings of Apostles, in faiths of Confessors,
in innocence of Holy Virgins, in deeds of righteous men.

I arise today through the strength of Heaven; light of Sun,
brilliance of Moon, splendor of Fire,
speed of Lightning, swiftness of Wind, depth of Sea,
stability of Earth, firmness of Rock.

I arise today through God's strength to pilot me,
God's might to uphold me,
God's wisdom to guide me,
God's eye to look before me,
God's ear to hear me,
God's word to speak for me,
God's hand to guard me,
God's way to lie before me,

God's shield to protect me,
God's host to secure me:
against snares of devils,
against temptations of vices,
against inclinations of nature,

against everyone who shall wish me ill,
afar and anear, alone and in a crowd.

I summon today all these powers between me (and these evils):
against every cruel and merciless power that
may oppose my body and my soul,
against incantations of false prophets,
against black laws of heathenry,

against false laws of heretics,
against craft of idolatry,
against spells of witches, smiths and wizards,
against every knowledge that endangers man's body and soul.
Christ to protect me today against poisoning,
against burning, against drowning, against wounding,
so that there may come abundance in reward.

Christ with me,
Christ before me,
Christ behind me,
Christ in me,
Christ beneath me,
Christ above me,
Christ on my right,
Christ on my left,

Christ in breadth,
Christ in length,
Christ in height,
Christ in the heart of every man who thinks of me,
Christ in the mouth of every man who speaks of me,

Christ in every eye that sees me,
Christ in every ear that hears me.

I arise today through a mighty strength,
the invocation of the Trinity,
through belief in the Threeness,
through confession of the Oneness of the Creator of creation.
Salvation is of the Lord.
Salvation is of the Lord.
Salvation is of Christ.
May Thy Salvation, O Lord, be ever with us.
Amen..

- Saint Patrick, 433 AD

May We All Be Safe From Sorrow

May all beings have happiness and the causes of happiness;
May all be free from sorrow and the causes of sorrow;
May all never be separated from the sacred happiness which is
sorrowless;
And may all live in equanimity, without too much attachment and

too much aversion,
And live believing in the equality of all that lives.

- Traditional Buddhist Prayer

Novena to Saint Jude

Saint Jude, glorious apostle, faithful servant and friend of Jesus, the name of the traitor has caused you to be forgotten by many. But the Church honors and invokes you universally as the patron of difficult and desperate cases. Pray for me, who am so miserable. Make use, I implore you, of that particular privilege accorded to you to bring visible and speedy help where help was almost despaired of. Come to my assistance in this great need that I may receive the consolation and help of heaven in all my necessities, tribulations, and sufferings, particularly — (here make your request) — and that I may bless God with you and all the elect throughout all eternity.

I promise you, O blessed Saint Jude, to be ever mindful of this great favor,

and I will never cease to honor you as my special and powerful patron

and do all in my power to encourage devotion to you. Amen..

Saint Jude, pray for us and for all who honor you and invoke your aid.

- National Shrine to St. Jude, Patron of Desperate Situations

Comforting Women With Breast Cancer

Father, for the strength you have given me, I thank you. For the
health you have blessed me with, I thank you. For the women who
are going through breast cancer and their families, I ask you to
strengthen and to heal as you see fit. Lord, we know you want us to
be in good health and to prosper. Lord, use us to do the work you
have for us to do. For we know time is getting short on this earth.
Lord, be with every woman who is sick and encourage them as only
you can. I know how faithful you are. You have shown yourself to
be everything you say you are in your Holy Word. I praise you, for
you made this body, and you can heal this body. In Jesus' Name
I pray.

- Fran Leffler, Las Vegas Women's Prayer Circle

Seek and Ye Shall Find

Ask, and it shall be given you;
Seek, and you shall find;
Knock, and it shall be opened to you.
For whoever asks, receives;
And he who seeks, finds;
And to him who knocks, the door is opened.

- Matthew 7:7, The Words of Christ, NIV

Prayer to Heal the Body

Beloved Lord, Almighty God,
Through the Rays of the Sun,
Through the Waves of the Air,
Through the All Pervading Life in Space;
Purify and Revivify Us
And we pray, heal our bodies, hearts, and souls.
Amen..

- Nayaz, Pir-o-murshid Inayat Khan

Calling Upon God the Great

I bow to Him who has conquered fear,
conquered all afflictions, conquered sensual vexation,
conquered passion, emotions, attachment, aversion and delusion,
and has conquered pleasure and pain.
May my misery end and the Karmic forces be annihilated.
May I attain enlightenment and meet a peaceful death.
May thy feet, O Noble Jina, the friend of all living beings,
be my happy refuge!

- Jain Namakar Mantra

God is Within Us All

May all I say and all I think
be in harmony with Thee,
God within me, God beyond me,
Maker of the Trees.

- Chinook Chant, Native North American

Your Gifts to the World

May I be protector for those without one,
A guide for all travelers on the way;
May I be a bridge, a boat and a ship
For all who wish to cross (the water).

May I be an island for those who seek one
And a lamp for those desiring light,
May I be a bed for all who wish to rest
And a slave for all who want a slave.

May I be a wishing jewel, a magic vase,
Powerful mantras and great medicine,
May I become a wish-fulfilling tree
And a cow of plenty for the world.

And the great elements such as earth,
May I always support the life
Of all the boundless creatures.

And until they pass away from pain
May I also be the source of life
For all the realms of varied beings
That reach unto the ends of space.

- Shantideva, India 760 AD

One Meaningful Word

Better
than if there were thousands
of meaningless words is
one
meaningful
word
that on hearing
brings peace.

Better
than if there were thousands
of meaningless verses is
one
meaningful
verse
that on hearing
brings peace.

And better than chanting hundreds
of meaningless verses is
one

Dhamma-saying
that on hearing
brings peace.

- Dhammapada; ascribed to Buddha

Eternal Love for All in the World

For as long as space endures
And for as long as living beings remain
Until then may I too abide
To dispel the misery of the world.

- Shantideva

Prayer for the Weary, Broken, and Afraid

Benedict, when the storm rages
around me,
and I can hold on no more,
when the waves of fear engulf me
and I am weary,
battered and sore,
take me then and steer me
storm-tossed, broken and afraid,
into the arms of your safe harbor
safely home.

- Prayer to St. Benedict

For Those Who Serve in the Military

Gracious God, we give thanks for military men and women, both
from the past and present, and for their courageous service and
sacrifice to our country and its people to secure the blessings of
life, liberty, and justice for all. May our remembrance be a timely
reminder that our freedom was purchased at high cost, and should
not be taken for granted. Give us resolve to labor in faithful service
to you until all share the benefits of freedom, justice, and peace;
through Jesus Christ our Lord. Amen.

- Episcopal Diocese of Fort Worth

For the Good of All

He who has subdued his passions and desires,
Who has realized the secret of the Universe in entirety;
Who has discoursed upon the teachings of the Right Path of
Liberation
For the benefit of all in a quite unselfish manner;
Who is variously termed Buddha, Mahavira, Jina,
Hari, Hara, Brahma and Self;
In Him, imbued with deep devotion,
May this mind (of mine) eternally dwell!

Those who have no longings left for sense-produced pleasures;
Who are rich in the quality of equanimity?
Who are day and night engaged in encompassing
The good of all—their own as well as of others?
Who undergo the severe penance of self-effacement

Without flinching—such Enlightened Saints
Verily conquer the pain and misery of mundane existence!

May I always associate with such aforesaid Holy men;
May my mind be constantly occupied with their contemplation;
May the longing of my heart be always to tread in their footsteps;
May I also never cause pain to any living being;
May I never utter untruth; and
May I never covet the wealth or wife or husband of another!
May I ever drink the nectar of contentment!

With pride may I never be elated, angry may I feel with none;
The sight of another's luck may not make me envious with his lot:
May my desire be for dealings fair and straight, and
May my heart only delight in doing good to others
To the best of my abilities all the days of my life!

May I always entertain a feeling of friendliness for
All living beings in the world;
May the spring of sympathy in my heart be ever bubbling

For those in agony and affliction;
May I never feel angry with the vile, the vicious and wrongly-
directed;
May there be such an adjustment of things
That I should always remain tranquil in dealing with them!

May my heart ever overflow with love at the sight of virtuous men;
May this mind of mine rejoice always in serving them to the
utmost of its power;
May I be never ungrateful;

May jealousies never approach me;
May my longing be always for assimilating the virtues of other; and
May the eyes never alight on their faults!

Whether people speak of me well or ill;
Whether wealth comes to me or departs;

Whether I live to be hundreds of thousands of years old;
Or give up the ghost this day;
Whether any one holds out any kind of fear;
Or with worldly riches tempts me;
In face of all these possible things
May my footsteps swerve not from the path of Truth!

With pleasure may the mind be not puffed up;
Let pain disturb it never;
May the awesome loneliness of a mountain, forest or river,
Or a burning place, never cause it to shiver;
Unmoved, unshakable, in firmness may it grow adamantine;
And display true moral strength when parted
From the desired thing, or united with what is undesired!

May happiness be the lot of all;
May distress come near none;

Giving up hatred, sin and pride;
May the world pour forth one continuous eternal peal of delight;
May Dharma become the main topic of conversation in every
household;
May evil cease to be easily wrought;

By increase of wisdom and merit of works,
May men realize the purpose of human life-Liberation (Moksha)!

May distress and suffering no longer exist;
May it rain in time;
May the king also be righteously inclined, and
Impartially administer justice to the subjects;
May disease, epidemics and famines cease;
May people live in peace;
May the exalted Ahimsa Dharma,
Religion of non-violence, prevail;
And the Gospel of mercy become the source of good to all!

May there be mutual love in the world;
May delusion dwell at a distance;
May no one ever utter unpleasant speech or words
That are harsh, with his tongue;
May men, heroes of the time,
Whole-heartedly work in their country's cause;
May all understand the Laws of Truth and
Joyfully sorrow and suffering endure!
Amen.!

Om, Peace, Shanti! Shanti! Shanti!

- Shri Jugal Kishor Mukhtyarji, 1864

A Guide For Those Who Have Lost Their Way

May I become at all times, both now and forever
A protector for those without protection
A guide for those who have lost their way
A ship for those with oceans to cross
A bridge for those with rivers to cross
A sanctuary for those in danger
A lamp for those without light
A place of refuge for those who lack shelter
And a servant to all in need.

- Buddhist Prayer of Peace

Help Me Now in My Urgent Need

O Holy St. Jude!

Apostle and Martyr,
great in virtue and rich in miracles,
near kinsman of Jesus Christ,
faithful intercessor for all who invoke you,
special patron in time of need;
to you I have recourse from the depth of my heart,
and humbly beg you,
to whom God has given such great power,
to come to my assistance;
help me now in my urgent need and grant my earnest petition.

I will never forget thy graces and favors you obtain for me
and I will do my utmost to spread devotion to you.

Amen.

St. Jude, pray for us and all who honor thee and invoke thy aid.

(Say 3 Our Fathers, 3 Hail Mary, and 3 Glory Be)

- Novena to St. Jude

You Will Have a Little Peace

Do everything with a mind that lets go.
Do not expect any praise or reward.
If you let go a little, you will have a little peace.
If you let go a lot, you will have a lot of peace.
If you let go completely, you will know complete peace and
freedom.
Your struggles with the world
will have come to an end.

- Achaan Chah, Thai Buddhist Monk, 1955

Morning Prayer

O Infinite God of life, goodness, and generous
love, I dedicate my heart, my life, to you.

Help me to cherish all human life,
and do the good you want me to do.

Make me a loving example of your generous love,
and a blessing to everyone I see.

May your goodness be fully in us,
and in all that we think and say and do.

- St. Francis of Assisi

Prayer for Any Time

O God, may I find and praise your goodness
dwelling within every human being.

May I be a living sign of your generous love,
and help everyone to live more intimately with you.

May we respect the evolving nature of all creation,
and grow to our fullness of life with you.

Guide our search into our entire human nature,
and into all creation, to know what you want us to do.

- Sacred Heart Catholic Church, UK

Evening Prayer

O God, Mary and Joseph cooperated with you
in the childhood training of Jesus.

May we cooperate with you when we help our friends,
our enemies, criminals, and everyone in need.
Help us do what we cannot do now.

May we cooperate with you for genuine justice
and peace in all that we think and say and do.

May we with Mary and Joseph follow Jesus, and share
your generous love with all the people of the world.

- Sacred Heart Catholic Church

Late Night Prayer

We praise you, O Infinite God of all life,
all existence, and all goodness.

We thank you for sharing your life and goodness
so freely with us and making us one with you.

We are sorry for harm that we have done, neglecting the
needy and resisting your loving presence.

Forgive us our sins. Help us mend the harm that we have
done. Save us from evil. Lead us to eternal life.

- Robert Leffler, Morning Star Church, West Virginia

Prayer for the Right Path

Doing the right thing is our best gift
That is what brings us bliss and happiness.
Happy and blissful is the person who does what is right,
because it is the right thing to do.

- Ancient Zoroastrian Chant

Blessings for the Afflicted

I desire neither earthly kingdom,
nor even freedom from birth and death.
I desire only the deliverance from grief
of all those afflicted by misery.
Oh Lord, lead us from the unreal to the real;
from darkness to light;
from death to immortality.
May there be peace in celestial regions.
May there be peace on earth.
May the waters be appeasing.
May herbs be wholesome and
may trees and plants bring peace to all.

May all beneficent beings bring peace to us.
May thy wisdom spread peace all through the world.
May all things be a source of peace to all and to me.
Om Shanti, Shanti, Shanti.

- Patricia Morrison, Crane Dance Collective, 1956

What God Sows In the Heart

Give over thine own willing;
give over thine own running;
give over thine own desiring
to know or to be anything;
and sink down to the seed
which God sows in the heart,
and let that grow in thee,
and be in thee,
and breathe in thee,
and act in thee,
and thou shalt find by sweet experience
that the Lord knows that,
and loves and owns that,
and will lead it to
the inheritance of life,
which is its portion.

- Isaac Pennington, 1661

An Irish Prayer

May God give you

For every storm, a rainbow

For each tear, a smile

For every care, a promise

And a blessing in each trial.

A faithful friend to share,

For every sigh, a sweet song,

And an answer for each prayer.

May the blessing of God's soft rain be on you.

- From Irish Oral Tradition

God's Blessing Will Always Be Upon You

May the blessing of God's soft rain be on you,
Falling gently on your head, refreshing your soul
With the sweetness of little flowers newly blooming.
May the strength of the winds of Heaven bless you,
Carrying the rain to wash your spirit clean
Sparkling after in the sunlight.
May the blessing of God's earth be on you,
And as you walk the roads,

May you always have a kind word
for those you meet.

- Traditional Irish Blessing

March

A Season of Change

"Prosperity is a great teacher; adversity is a greater."
—William Hazlitt

"Hope is important because it can make the present moment less difficult to bear. If we believe that tomorrow will be better, we can bear a hardship today."
—Thich Nhat Hanh

"Problems are not stop signs, they are guidelines."
—Robert Schuller

"Prosperity is not without many fears and disasters; and adversity is not without comforts and hopes."
—Francis Bacon

Shine the Light of Love

May the blessing of light be upon you.

May the blessing of light be upon you,
Light on the outside,
Light on the inside.

With God's sunlight shining on you,
May your heart glow with warmth,
Like a turf fire
that welcomes friends and strangers alike.

May the light of the Lord shine from your eyes,
Like a candle in the window,
Welcoming the weary traveler.

—Traditional Irish Blessing

Irish Travelers Blessing

May the Hand of a Friend Always Be Near You
May there always be work for your hands to do;
May your purse always hold a coin or two;
May the sun always shine on your windowpane;
May a rainbow be certain to follow each rain;
May the hand of a friend always be near you;
May God fill your heart with gladness to cheer you.

- Traditional Irish Blessing

Never Give Up

I will not die an unlived life.
I will not live in fear
of falling or catching fire.
I choose to inhabit my days,
to allow my living to open me,
to make me less afraid,
more accessible,
to loosen my heart
until it becomes a wing.

- Dawna Markova

We Are All In This Together

All human beings are limbs of each other,
having been created of one essence.

When time affects a limb with pain,
The other limbs cannot at rest remain.

If thou feel not others' misery,
A human being is no name for thee.

- Sa'adi, Persian Poet, 1270

Asking Forgiveness

O little self, within whose smallness lies
All that man was, and is, and will become,
Atom unseen that comprehends the skies
And tells the tracks by which the planets roam;
That, without moving, knows the joys of wings,
The tiger's strength, the eagle's secrecy,
And in the hovel can consort with kings,
Or clothe a god with his own mystery.
O with what darkness do we cloak thy light,
What dusty folly gather thee for food,
Thou who alone art knowledge and delight,
The heavenly bread, the beautiful, the good.
O living self, O god, O morning star,
Give us thy light, forgive us what we are.

- John Masefield, 1915

Keep Me Safe Forever

Bless, O Mistress of Magic,
Myself and everything anear me,
Bless me in all my makings,
And keep me safe forever.

Keep me safe forever.

From every unclean spirit and sending,
From every evil wish and cursing,

From every wicked spell and glamour,
From every star that frowns upon me,
Save me till the end of my day.
That they may keep me safe forever.

Save me till the end of my day.

Let every nymph and faerie be my sister,
Let every troll and brownie be my brother,
Let every fairy-mouse and will-o-the-wisp befriend me,
That they may keep me safe forever.

That they may keep me safe forever.

- Ancient Celtic Oral Tradition

What Is Your Gift to the World?

May the gift I give
change me and our world.

- Reverend Alan Claassen, 2011

Call Upon Your Inner Strength, No Matter What

If you hear the dogs,
keep on going.

If you hear gunfire,
keep on going.

If you hear shouts and footsteps,
keep on going.

- Harriet Tubman

Be Gentle and Kind to Yourself

You're not alone.
So long as you reach out to others you're never alone.
Ask for my help in loaning you the courage you already have.
It's not that I never give you more than you can handle,
I am not responsible for the consequences of your actions,
only you are. Stay on the path of you're suffering
by taking the steps you need to take.
Hang on and hang in there, because it's now
that you're growing at light speed,
You're never going backward, only forward.

Decay your loneliness, by making full use
of my greatest gift to mankind, which is mankind.
Feel my alleged absence as proof,
for the paradox that I exist and have always existed.
Let me in by letting me out.

Love, fear, and all of the other feelings spared
are what create this reality.
These are the cause and effect of compassion and true forgiveness.

Ask for my help in walking through the anguish of forgiveness.
Do everything in your power to learn to forgive
and love those that hurt you,

Not for just them, but for others as well as yourself.
And never give up the hope that someday your ex-suffering
will be able to help the ones who were sick and hurt you,
As well as those who suffered like you.
Learn all this by practicing to love everyone.

Always look into yourself first;
your past, your present, your motives,
your feelings, and share the secrets
you find with myself as well as others.
Be gentle and kind to yourself
by being vulnerable, and sharing yourself
with others who are patient, kind, and who can only
try to love and accept you as much as I do.
As you get better at this,
take the risks that will enable you to venture out
further and further, so that your true self
may finally be exposed to the real world
I created for you to live in.

Be honest with everyone by never
accepting the blame that is not yours.
Free yourself with the truth, by telling
those stepping on your toes how you feel,
no matter how difficult it may seem at first, or
what its consequences may be;
you'll only get better at it.

If you can learn to love, forgive,
fully listen, understand, and accept those around you,
you will eventually begin to learn how to love, forgive,
fully listen, understand, and accept yourself.

- Anonymous

Lead Us To Light And Truth

Asatho Maa Sad Gamaya.
Thamaso Maa Jyothir Gamaya.
Mrithyur Maa Amritham Gamaya.
Om Shanti, Shanti, Shanti.

From untruth lead us to Truth.
From darkness lead us to Light.
From death lead us to Immortality.
Om Peace, Peace, Peace.

- Ancient Vedic Prayer

Embrace Humility, Patience, and Love

O Lord and Master of my life,
take from me the spirit of sloth, despondency,
lust of power, and idle talk;

But grant rather
the spirit of chastity, humility, patience, and love
to thy servant.

Yea, O Lord and King,
grant to me to see my own transgressions,
and not to judge my brother;
for blessed art Thou unto the ages of ages.

- Syriac Christian Prayer of St. Ephrem, 353

Be Filled With Deep And Abiding Peace

Deep peace I breathe into you,

O weariness, here:
O ache, here!

Deep peace, a soft white dove to you;
Deep peace, a quiet rain to you;
Deep peace, an ebbing wave to you!
Deep peace, red wind of the east from you;
Deep peace, grey wind of the west to you;
Deep peace, dark wind of the north from you;
Deep peace, blue wind of the south to you!
Deep peace, pure red of the flame to you;
Deep peace, pure white of the moon to you;
Deep peace, pure green of the grass to you;
Deep peace, pure brown of the earth to you;
Deep peace, pure grey of the dew to you,

Deep peace, pure blue of the sky to you!
Deep peace of the running wave to you,
Deep peace of the flowing air to you.

- Anonymous

What Is Your Service to the World?

God,

I'm willing
to do your work.

Please
show me what it is.

- Tami Simon, Boulder, Colorado

Everything Is Beautiful

In the house made of dawn.
In the story made of dawn.
On the trail of dawn.
O, Talking God.
His feet, my feet, restore.
His limbs, my limbs, restore.
His body, my body, restore.
His voice, my voice, restore.
His plumes, my plumes, restore.

With beauty before him, with beauty before me.
With beauty behind him, with beauty behind me.
With beauty above him, with beauty above me.
With beauty below him, with beauty below me.
With beauty around him, with beauty around me.
With pollen beautiful in his voice,
with pollen beautiful in my voice. It is finished in beauty.
It is finished in beauty.
In the house of evening light.
From the story made of evening light.
On the trail of evening light.

- Navajo Prayer

All Roads Lead to the Same Great Truth

I believe in the fundamental truth of all
great religions of the world.

I believe that they are all God-given
and I believe that they were necessary

for the people to whom these religions were revealed.
And I believe that if only we could all of us
read the scriptures of the different faiths from the standpoints
of the followers of these faiths,
we should find that they were at bottom
all one and were all helpful to one another.

- Mahatma Gandhi

Compassion for All Who Suffer

Satveshu Maitrim Gunishu Pramodham
Klishteshu Jivehu Krupa Parathvam
Madhyastha Bhavam Viparita Vruthow
Sada Mamatma Viddhatu Deva

O Lord! Make myself such that I may have love for all beings,
Joy in the meritorious, unstinted sympathy for the distressed
And tolerance towards the perversely inclined.

O Lord! May my soul always find fulfillment, in friendship and love
towards all beings,
In all the virtuous, in compassion toward all suffering creatures,
And in remaining neutral towards those hostile to me.
This is my prayer.

- Ancient Jain Prayer of Love for All

When You're Broken Open

Dance, when you're broken open.
Dance, if you've torn the bandage off.
Dance in the middle of the fighting.
Dance in your blood.
Dance, when you're perfectly free.

- Jelaluddin Rumi

Strength, Hope, Courage, and Love

Disturb us, Lord, when
We are too well pleased with ourselves,
When our dreams have come true
Because we have dreamed too little,
When we arrived safely
Because we sailed too close to the shore.

Disturb us, Lord, when
With the abundance of things we possess
We have lost our thirst
For the waters of life;
Having fallen in love with life,
We have ceased to dream of eternity
And in our efforts to build a new earth,
We have allowed our vision
Of the new Heaven to dim.

Disturb us, Lord, to dare more boldly,
To venture on wider seas
Where storms will show your mastery;
Where losing sight of land,
We shall find the stars.

We ask You to push back
The horizons of our hopes;
And to push into the future
In strength, courage, hope, and love.

- Daily Prayer [1941]

Before the Cross

O My Father, if it is possible,
let this cup pass from Me;
nevertheless, not as I will,
but as You will.

Again, a second time, He went away and prayed, saying,

O My Father, if this cup
cannot pass away from Me
unless I drink it,
Your will be done.

- Matthew 26:39-42, Jesus' Prayer in the Garden of Gethsemane,
NSV.

Practice Random Acts of Kindness

Be kind,
for everyone
you meet
is fighting
a hard
battle.

- Ian Maclaren, 1898

For The Little Children

Father-Mother God,
Loving me,
Guard me when I sleep;
Guide my little feet
Up to Thee.

- Mary Baker Eddy

Suffer Us Not

Blessed sister, holy mother,
spirit of the fountain, spirit of the garden,
Suffer us not to mock ourselves with falsehood
Teach us to care and not to care
Teach us to sit still
Even among these rocks,
Our peace in His will
And even among these rocks
Sister, mother,
And spirit of the river, spirit of the sea,
Suffer me not to be separated
And let my cry come unto Thee.

- Ash Wednesday, T.S. Eliot; 1927

Prayer for the Unity of All Peoples

God grant that the light of unity
may envelop the whole earth,
and that the seal, "The Kingdom is God's"
may be stamped upon the brow of all its peoples.

- Bahá'í. Bahá'u'lláh

Eulogy For Martyred Children

Our Lord! Condemn us not if we forget and fall into error;
Our Lord! Lay not on us a burden
like that which Thou didst lay on those before us;
Our Lord! Lay not on us a burden greater
than we have the strength to bear.
Blot out our sins, and grant us forgiveness.
Have mercy on us.
Thou art our protector;
Help us against those who stand against Faith.

- Dr. Martin Luther King, Jr.

How To Pray

Jesus taught that effective prayer must be:

Unselfish — not alone for oneself.

Believing — according to faith.

Sincere — honest of heart.

Intelligent — according to light.

Trustful — in submission to the Father's all-wise will.

- The Urantia Book: 144:3

The Only Thing That Matters

I do not think that the measure of a civilization
is how tall its buildings of concrete are,
but rather how well its people have learned to relate
to their environment and fellow man.

- Sun Bear, Chippewa Medicine Man

God Is Good

Cast me not away from thy presence;
and take not thy holy spirit from me.

Restore unto me the joy of thy salvation;
and uphold me with thy free spirit.

- Psalm 51: 11-12, King David, KJV

Let Me Lift Your Heavy Burdens and Give You Rest

Jesus said, "Come to me, all of you who are weary and carry heavy burdens, and I will give you rest. Take my yoke upon you. Let me teach you, because I am humble and gentle, and you will find rest for your souls. For my yoke fits perfectly, and the burden I give you is light."

- Matthew 11:28-30, NTL.

Cheer the Heart with Pure Love

Help them, O God, in their endeavor,
and grant them strength to serve Thee. O God!
Leave them not to themselves
but guide their steps by the light of Thy knowledge,
and cheer their hearts by Thy love.
Verily, Thou art their Helper and their Lord.

- Baha'i Prayer

I Say a Little Prayer For You

A little prayer enters my mind
Asking for inspiration
For guidance and peace

Creative forces, floating in air
Tainted with love from within
Miraculous blend

A vision of a wonderful world
A dream...
No, it is real.

- Hans van Rostenberghe

Small Wonder

We are alive in a fearsome time,
and we have been given new things to fear.

We've been delivered huge blows but also
huge opportunities to reinforce or reinvent our will,
depending on where we look for honor
and how we name our enemies.

The easiest thing is to think of returning the blows.
But there are other things we must think about as well,
other dangers we face.

The changes we dread most may contain our salvation.

- Barbara Kingsolver

April

Blossoming Into Being

"The trick is to enjoy life. Don't wish away your days, waiting for better ones ahead."
—Marjorie Pay Hinckley

"Nobody can make you feel inferior without your consent."
—Eleanor Roosevelt

"The greatest mistake you can make in life is to continually fear that you will make one."
—Elbert Hubbard

"Be miserable. Or motivate yourself. Whatever has to be done, it's always your choice."
—Wayne Dyer

Gimme Shelter

Let me not pray to be sheltered from dangers
but to be fearless in facing them.

Let me not beg for the stilling of my pain
but for the heart to conquer it.

Let me not look for allies in life's battlefield
but to my own strength.

Let me not crave in anxious fear to be saved
but hope for the patience to win my freedom.

Grant that I may not be a coward,
feeling Your mercy in my success alone;

But let me find the grasp of Your hand in my failure.

- Rabindranath Tagore, 1916

Keep Us from Evil

Father, the hour is come; glorify thy Son,
that thy Son also may glorify thee:

As thou hast given him power over all flesh,
that he should give eternal life to as many as thou hast given him.

And this is life eternal, that they might know thee
the only true God, and Jesus Christ, whom thou hast sent.

I have glorified thee on the earth:
I have finished the work which thou gavest me to do.

And now, O Father, glorify thou me with thine own self
with the glory which I had with thee before the world was.

I have manifested thy name unto the men
which thou gavest me out of the world:

thine they were, and thou gavest them me;
and they have kept thy word.

Now they have known that all things
whatsoever thou hast given me are of thee.

For I have given unto them the words which thou gavest me;
and they have received them,
and have known surely that I came out from thee,
and they have believed that thou didst send me.

I pray for them: I pray not for the world,
but for them which thou hast given me; for they are thine.

And all mine are thine, and thine are mine;
and I am glorified in them.

And now I am no more in the world,
but these are in the world, and I come to thee.
Holy Father, keep through thine own name
those whom thou hast given me, that they may be one, as we are.

While I was with them in the world, I kept them in thy name:
those that thou gavest me I have kept, and none of them is lost,
but the son of perdition; that the scripture might be fulfilled.

And now come I to thee; and these things I speak in the world,
that they might have my joy fulfilled in themselves.

I have given them thy word; and the world hath hated them,
because they are not of the world, even as I am not of the world.

Pray not that thou shouldst take them out of the world,
but that thou shouldst keep them from evil.

They are not of the world, even as I am not of the world.

Sanctify them through thy truth: thy word is truth.

As thou hast sent me into the world, even so
have I also sent them into the world.

And for their sakes I sanctify myself,
that they also might be sanctified through the truth.

Neither pray I for these alone, but for them
also which shall believe on me through their word;

That they all may be one; as thou, Father, art in me, and I in thee,
that they also may be one in us:
that the world may believe that thou hast sent me.

And the glory which thou gavest me I have given them;
that they may be one, even as we are one:

I in them, and thou in me, that they may be made perfect in one;
and that the world may know that thou hast sent me,
and hast loved them, as thou hast loved me.

Father, I whom thou hast given me, be with me where I am;
that they may behold my glory, which thou hast given me:
for thou didst love me before the foundation of the world.

O righteous Father, the world hath not known thee:
but I have known thee,
and these have known that thou hast sent me.

And I have declared unto them thy name, and will declare it:
that the love wherewith thou hast loved me
may be in them, and I in them.

- St. John 17, the words of Jesus Christ
Make Peace, Not War

Children, everybody, here's what to do during war:

In a time of destruction, create something.
A poem.
A parade.
A community.
A school.
A vow.

A moral principle.
One peaceful moment.

- Maxine Hong Kingston, The Fifth Book of Peace

Let Nothing Disturb Thee

Nada te turbe,
Nada te espante,
Toda se pasa,
Dios no se muda,
La Paciencia
Todo la alcanza.
Quien a Dios tiene
Nada le falta:
Sólo Dios basta.

Let nothing disturb thee;
Let nothing dismay thee;
All things pass:
God never changes.
Patience attains

All that it strives for.
He who has God
Lacks for nothing:
God alone suffices.

- St. Teresa of Avila, 16th Century

Chant for the Sacred Earth

Cover my earth mother four times with many flowers.
Let the heavens be covered with the banked-up clouds.
Let the earth be covered with fog;
cover the earth with rains.
Great waters, rains, cover the earth.
Lightning cover the earth.
Let thunder be heard over the earth;
let thunder be heard;
Let thunder be heard over the six regions of the earth.

- Native American Oral Tradition

Plea to He Who is All-Knowing

Oh Allah!
I consult You as You are all-knowing,
and I seek ability from Your power and I ask You for Your great
favor,
for You have power,
but I do not,
and You have knowledge,
but I do not,
and You know all hidden matters.

Oh Allah!
If You know that this matter is good for me in my religion,
my livelihood and my life in the Hereafter,
then make it easy and bless it;

and if You know that this matter is evil for me in my religion,
my livelihood and my life in the Hereafter,
then keep it away from me and keep me away from it,
and choose what is good for me wherever it is, and make me
pleased with it.

- Prophet Muhammad

Perfect Be Our Unity

Let us be united;
Let us speak in harmony;
Let our minds apprehend alike.
Common be our prayer,
Common be the end of our assembly;
Common be our resolution;
Common be our deliberations.
Alike be our feelings;
Unified be our hearts;
Common be our intentions;
Perfect be our unity.

- The Rig-Veda

Prayer For Protection From All Danger

Circle me, Lord.
Keep protection near
And danger afar.

Circle me, Lord
Keep hope within.
Keep doubt without.

Circle me, Lord.
Keep light near
And darkness afar.

Circle me, Lord.
Keep peace within.
Keep evil out.

- Coptic Christian Blessing

Warrior's Creed

I have no parents:
I make the heaven and earth my parents.

I have no home:
I make awareness my home.

I have no life and death:
I make the tides of breathing my life and death.

I have no divine powers:
I make honesty my divine power.

I have no means:
I make understanding my means.

I have no secrets:
I make character my secret.

I have no body:
I make endurance my body.

I have no eyes:
I make the flash of lightning my eyes.

I have no ears:
I make sensibility my ears.

I have no limbs:
I make promptness my limbs.

I have no strategy:
I make "unshadowed by thought" my strategy.

I have no design:
I make "seizing opportunity by the forelock" my design.

I have no miracles:
I make right action my miracle.

I have no principles:
I make adaptability to all circumstances my principle.

I have no tactics:
I make emptiness and fullness my tactics.

I have no talent:
I make ready with my talent.

I have no friends:
I make my mind my friend.

I have no enemy:
I make carelessness my enemy.

I have no armor:
I make benevolence and righteousness my armor.

I have no castle:
I make immovable mind my castle.

I have no sword:
I make absence of self my sword.

- Anonymous Samurai Song—14th Century

Remember the Ways of Truth and Love in Times of Despair

When I despair,
I remember that all through history
the ways of truth and love have always won.
There have been tyrants, and murderers,

and for a time they can seem invincible,
but in the end they always fall.

Think of it—always.

- *Mahatma Gandhi*

Prayer to St. Peregrine, Patron Saint of Cancer Patients

O great St. Peregrine, you have been called "The Mighty," "The Wonder-Worker," because of the numerous miracles which you have obtained from God for those who have had recourse to you. For so many years you bore in your own flesh this cancerous disease that destroys the very fiber of our being, and had recourse to the source of all grace when the power of man could do no more. You were favored with the vision of Jesus coming down from His Cross to heal your affliction. Ask of God and Our Lady the cure of the sick whom we entrust to you. (Pause here and silently recall the names of the sick for whom you are praying.) Aided in this way by your powerful intercession, we shall sing to God, now and for all eternity, a song of gratitude for His great goodness and mercy.

Amen..

- *Anonymous*

In Times of Great Sadness

Dear God, After the sadness I didn't think I could ever be the same again. I was right. I now have qualities I never had before. I am more sensitive to the sorrows of others. I am more compassionate to the less fortunate. I appreciate deeply. I love more intensely. Thank You for giving me the wisdom that comes from life experiences.

Amen.

- Martha Lynn, Harmony Hollows

Prayer for the Illumination and Light

O Thou Who art generous and merciful!
We are the servants of Thy threshold and are gathered
beneath the sheltering shadow of Thy divine unity.
The sun of Thy mercy is shining upon all,
and the clouds of Thy bounty shower upon all.
Thy gifts encompass all,
Thy loving providence sustains all,
Thy protection overshadows all, and the glances of
Thy favor are cast upon all.
O Lord! Grant Thine infinite bestowals,
and let the light of Thy guidance shine.
Illumine the eyes, gladden the hearts with abiding joy.
Confer a new spirit upon all people and bestow upon them eternal
life.
Unlock the gates of true understanding

and let the light of faith shine resplendent.
Gather all people beneath the shadow of Thy bounty
and cause them to unite in harmony,
so that they may become as the rays of one sun,
as the waves of one ocean, and as the fruit of one tree.
May they be refreshed by the same breeze.
May they receive illumination from the same source of light.
Thou art the Giver, the Merciful, the Omnipotent.

- Byzantine Coptic Christian Prayer

God Is Our Hope

God is our hope and strength,
a very present help in trouble.

Therefore will we not fear, though the earth be moved,
and though the hills be carried into the midst of the sea;

Though the waters thereof rage and swell,
and though the mountains shake at the tempest of the same.

There is a river, the streams whereof make glad the city of God,
the holy place of the tabernacle of the Most High.

- Psalms 46:1-4, KJV

A Prayer for the Good of All People

Let us pray for all to be happy,
to love one another,
to help each other,
to gain wisdom,
for all to receive god's blessings,
to break free from the illusion
that is distracting us from our true nature.

No one shall go hungry,
no one will suffer,
abundance is with everyone
and all negativity shall be removed!

- Unitarian Universalist Blessing

Prayer for America

America needs religion.
Let it be preached, let it be taught, let it be practiced.

But while each of us goes our own way to the church of our choice,
free to worship as we will, and to declare our faith and to persuade
others,
let all of us together remember that democracy unites us in
spiritual communion,
and that we are citizens of one country just as we are children of
one God.

Let us not disdain our heritage.

There is a faith within democracy drawn from the best of
all religions.

It is a faith in the victory of truth in free and open encounters,
and in the triumph of liberty over servitude, and of universal over
provincial,
and of unity over exclusiveness, and love over fear.

Whatever may separate us in conviction, ritual, or devotion, let this
unite us.

Without it we are lost—and so is the hope of this world.

- Reverend A. Powell Davies, 1952

Call Upon the Saints to Heal and Help Us

Lord God, Giver of Life, Source of all healing,
who alone can help us grow in wholeness:
We thank you for the gift of life and health,
and remembering your faithful servants
Cosmus and Damian
we ask you to guide and uphold
all doctors, surgeons, hospital staffs, and
all engaged in the ministry of healing
together with those they serve,
that disease and disunity
may everywhere be overcome;

through Christ the Divine Healer,
who suffered and died and lives and reigns
with you and the Holy Spirit
our God of Salvation, now and always.
Amen..

- Parish Prayer, St. Cosmus & St. Damian

For Our Country

Almighty God, you have given us this good land for our heritage:

We humbly pray that we may always prove ourselves a people mindful of your favor and glad to do your will. Bless our land with honorable industry, sound learning, and pure manners. Save us from violence, discord, and confusion; from pride and arrogance, and from every evil way. Defend our liberties, and fashion into one united people the multitudes brought hither out of many kindreds and tongues. Endue with the spirit of wisdom those to whom in your Name we entrust the authority of government, that there may be justice and peace at home, and that through obedience to your law, we may show forth your praise among the nations of the earth. In the time of prosperity, fill our hearts with thankfulness, and in the day of trouble, suffer not our trust in you to fail; all which we ask through Jesus Christ our Lord. Amen..

- Guiding Star Church

Ask That Your Heart Be Filled

If you cannot refuse to fall down,
refuse to stay down.
If you cannot refuse to stay down
lift your heart toward heaven
and like a hungry beggar,
ask that it be filled,
and it will be filled.
You may be pushed down.
You may be kept from rising.
But no one can keep you
from lifting your heart
toward heaven —
only you.
It is in the midst of misery
that so much becomes clear.
The one who says nothing good
came of this,
is not yet listening.

- Clarissa Pinkola Estes

The Gift of Pure Heart

Create in me a pure heart, O God,
and renew a steadfast spirit within me.

Do not cast me from your presence
or take your Holy Spirit from me.

Restore to me the joy of salvation
and grant me a willing spirit to sustain me.

- Psalm 51:10-12—King David, NIT

To Be of Use

At the center of the universe is a
loving heart that continues to beat
and that wants the best for every person.

Anything we can do to help foster
the intellect and spirit and emotional growth
of our fellow human beings, that is our job.

Those of us who have this particular vision
must continue against all odds.

Life is for service.

- Fred Rogers of Mister Roger's Neighborhood, 1959

Let's Believe In Humankind

As I look around,
I see the crumbling ruins of civilization
like a vast heap of futility.

Yet I shall not commit
the grievous sin
of losing faith in man.

- Rabindranath Tagore, 1941

Today I Purpose to Live

My life will shine
As the morning sings
I walk in liberty
Bound in true dreams
Manifested promises
Chase my forward motion
A covered path before me
The fruits of my hoping
The fruits of my living

Today I purpose to love

My love will speak
With the sound of grace
Merciful within mercy

The works of my faith
Smiles of overflowing
Inspire my giving

Abundance of joy as rain
The fruits of my living

- Michael John Faciane

For Our Grandmothers Who Have Given So Much

We thank You, God, for all of the grandmothers who have given so much. Their love and wisdom have helped to shape us into who we are, and we have learned about how to love You and how to love each other through their example.

Bless each of them with long life and show us all how to honor them in ways that would let them know how much they mean to us that would also be pleasing in Your sight.

Amen..

- Kimberly Lynn Davis, Recovery Room

Send Thy Peace, O Lord

Send Thy peace, O Lord, that we
may endure all, tolerate all, in the thought of
Thy grace and mercy.

Send Thy peace, O Lord, that our lives
may become a Divine vision, and in Thy light,
all darkness may vanish.

Send Thy peace, O Lord, our Father and Mother,
that we Thy children on Earth
may all unite in one family.

- Pir-O-Murshid Inayat Khan, 1921

A Celtic Prayer

God to enfold me,
God to surround me,
God in my speaking,
God in my thinking.

God in my sleeping,
God in my waking,
God in my watching,
God in my hoping.

God in my life,
God in my lips,
God in my soul,
God in my heart.

God in my sufficing,
God in my slumber,

God in mine ever-living soul,
God in mine eternity.

- Ancient Celtic Oral Tradition

Come to Me Quickly, O Lord

Lord, I cry unto thee: make haste unto me;
give ear unto voice, when I cry unto thee.

Let my prayer be set forth before thee as incense;
and the lifting of my hands as the evening sacrifice.

- Psalm 141:1-2—King David

Beloved Jesus, Shine Through Me Today

Dear Jesus, help us to spread your fragrance everywhere we go.
Flood our souls with your spirit and life.
Penetrate and possess our whole being so utterly,
that our lives may only be a radiance of yours.
Shine through us, and be so in us,
that every person we should come in contact with
may feel your presence in our soul.
Let them look up and see no longer us, but only Jesus.
Stay with us, and then we shall begin to shine as you shine;
so to shine as to be a light to others;
the light, Jesus, will be all from you.
None of it will be ours.

It will be you shining on others through us.
Let us thus praise you in the way you love best,
by shining on those around us.
Let us preach you without preaching:

not by words, but by our example,
by the catching force,
the sympathetic influence of what we do,
the evident fullness of the love our hearts bear for you.
Amen..

- Dr. Jane Goodall's Favorite Prayer, by Mother Teresa

Think of Our Children

There will be no other words in the world
But those our children speak. What will she make of a world
Do you suppose, of which she is made?

- George Oppen

God Grant Me Grace to Be My Best Self

Give us the strength it takes
to listen rather than to judge,
to trust rather than to fear,
to try again and again
to make peace even when peace eludes us.

We ask, O God, for the grace
to be our best selves.
We ask for the vision
to be builders of the human community
rather than its destroyers.
We ask for the humility as a people
to understand the fears and hopes of other peoples.

We ask for the love it takes
to bequeath to the children of the world to come
more than the failures of our own making.
We ask for the heart it takes
to care for all the peoples

For You, O God, have been merciful to us.

For You, O God, have been patient with us.
For You, O God, have been gracious to us.

And so may we be merciful
and patient
and gracious
and trusting
with these others whom you also love.
This we ask through Jesus,
the one without vengeance in his heart.
This we ask forever and ever.

Amen.

- Benedictine Sisters' Prayer for World Peace

May

When Hope Springs Eternal

"Courage does not always roar. Sometimes courage is the quiet voice at the end of the day saying, 'I will try again tomorrow.'"
—Mary Anne Radmacher

"Always remember you are braver than you believe, stronger than you seem, smarter than you think, and twice as beautiful as you've ever imagined."
—Dr. Seuss

"Very little is needed to make a happy life; it is all within yourself, in your way of thinking."
—Marcus Aurelius

"Life isn't about getting and having, it's about giving and being."
—Kevin Kruse

Let Me Take Refuge in the Shelter of Your Wings

Hear my cry, O God;
listen to my prayer.
From the ends of the earth I call to you,
I call as my heart grows faint;
lead me to the rock that is higher than I.
For you have been my refuge,
a strong tower against the foe
I long to dwell in your tent forever
and take refuge in the shelter of your wings.

- Psalm of David, Psalm 61, 1-4, NIV

As I Lay Me Down to Sleep

Matthew, Mark, Luke and John,
The bed be blest that I lie on.

Four corners to my bed,
Four angels round my head;
One to watch, and one to pray,
And two to bear my soul away.

- 17th Century Child's Bedtime Prayer

Earth Prayer

May the waters flow peacefully; may the herbs and plants grow peacefully; may all the divine powers bring unto us peace. May the rain come down in the proper time, may the earth yield plenty of corn, may the country be free from war. The supreme Lord is peace.

- Hindu tradition

The Soul's Passage

Exultation is the going
Of an inland soul to sea,
Past the houses—past the headlands –
Into deep Eternity –

Bred as we, among the mountains,
Can the sailor understand
The divine intoxication
Of the first league out from land?

- Emily Dickinson

At the Breaking of the World, God's Power Heals With Love

Dear Lord, I may not see the sun and moon lose their light. I may not witness rivers turn red, or stars fall from the sky.

Yet there are times when my world becomes unhinged
and the foundations of what I believe crack and dissolve.
Give me the grace to believe that Your power is at work
in the turmoil of my life.
Lead me to remember that Your power is greater than all evil,
and though the world may rock and sometimes break,
it will in time be transformed by Your love.

- Anonymous

Prayer for a Sick Child

Lord Jesus Christ,

Good Shepherd of the sheep,

You gather the lambs in your arms

And carry them in your bosom.

We commend to your loving care this child, _____.

Relieve his/her pain; guard him/her from all danger,

Restore to him/her your gifts of gladness and strength,

And raise him/her up to a life of service to you.

Hear us, we pray, for dear [Name]' s sake. Amen..

- Anonymous

Pray Loud

Wage peace with your breath.
Breathe in firemen and rubble,
Breathe out whole buildings and flocks of red wing blackbirds
Breathe out sleeping children and freshly mown fields.
Breathe in confusion and breathe out maple trees.
Breathe in the fallen and breathe out lifelong friendships intact.
Wage peace with your listening: hearing sirens, pray loud.
Remember your tools: flower seeds, clothes pins, clean rivers.
Make soup.
Play music, memorize the words for thank you in three languages.

- Judyth Hill

Poem in Wartime

The straight and the square rarely advance
I'm serving in the stupidest of posts
I don't have time to open a book
buried beneath casework and records
the disaster of war has worn us all down
there's no vacation from corvée and taxes
the downtrodden masses need help
but compassionate measures only cause us trouble
I think of retiring day and night
from outside my door I can see the old mountains

if you feel the same
let's go back arm-in-arm together.

*- In Kaoling Describing My Feelings to Commandant Lu of
Sanyuan. —Wei Ying-wu*

Celebrating Life After the Hard Times

won't you celebrate with me
what i have shaped into
a kind of life? i had no model.
born in babylon
both nonwhite and woman
what did i see to be except myself?
i made it up
here on this bridge between
starshine and clay,
my one hand holding tight
my other hand; come celebrate
with me that everyday
something has tried to kill me
and has failed.

- Lucille Clifton

Poem Prayer for the End of All War

We interrupt this war for doctors to heal,
teachers to teach, and students to learn.

We interrupt this war to marvel at sunsets,
listen to music, and to laugh.

We interrupt this war for poets to rhyme, sculptors to
chisel, and writers to paint pictures with words.

We interrupt this war to plant tomatoes, mow
the grass, and to smell the roses.

We interrupt this war to feed the hungry, build
new schools, and to stamp out ignorance.

We interrupt this war to clean up the air, save
the whales and to find a cure for cancer.

- Cappy Hall Rearick

Let Us Live By The Spirit

But the fruit of the Spirit is love, joy, peace, patience, kindness,
goodness, faithfulness, gentleness, self-control; against such
things there is no law. If we live by the Spirit, let us also walk by
the Spirit.

- Galatians 5:22-25

In Hard and Mean Days

Father, Mother, God,
Thank you for your presence
during the hard and mean days.
For then we have you to lean upon.
Thank you for your presence
during the bright and sunny days,
for then we can share that which we have
with those who have less.

For those who have no voice,
we ask you to speak.
For those who feel unworthy,
we ask you to pour your love out
in waterfalls of tenderness.

- Maya Angelou

Blessings for the World

Blessed be the Earth and those who tend her,
for she is the source and sustenance of our lives.

Blessed be the children who hunger for food,
learning, and homes that are safe,
for their future is shaped by our choices today.

Blessed be the refugees fleeing the violence of war and poverty
may they find shelter, peace, and work that sustains them.

Blessed be those who are calling for freedom,
resisting oppression and risking their lives in the struggle for
justice,
for they are the shapers of a brighter world.

Blessed be the persecuted and wrongly judged,
for theirs is a sorrow lessened only by mercy and human kindness

Blessed be the prophets who speak and write of a world beyond
war,
for theirs are the words becoming flesh.

Blessed be the story-tellers, music-makers, and artists of life,
for they are the true light of the world.

Blessed be the tender-hearted who mourn and grieve
the wars we've fought, the lives we've lost,
may peace ride in on the river of their tears.

- Louise Harmon

May the Grace of Transfiguration Heal You

May you know tender shelter and healing blessing

when you are called to stand in the place of pain.
May the places of darkness within you be surprised by light.
May you be granted the wisdom to avoid false resistance,

and when suffering knocks on the door of your life,

may you be able to glimpse its hidden gift.
May you be able to see the fruits of suffering.
May memory bless and shelter you with the hard-earned light of
past turmoil,

to remind you that you have survived before,
And though the darkness is now deep,
You will soon see approaching light.
May this give you confidence and trust.
May a window of light always surprise you.
May the grace of transfiguration heal your wounds.

- John O'Donohue

Helping Those Who Help Themselves

At the depths of despair, nothing matters, I can't do anything, got
to get out of here, walls falling in, throw me a rope, I can't move,
can't stand it, nothing, throw me a rope...

And one day, like any other day, finally tired of waiting for help
that never comes, make a rope, tie it to a rock throw it up pull
yourself out and walk away...

And it took all that time
just to find yourself.

And that's how long it had to take;
and it was well worth every moment.

- Paul Williams

Through These Our Hands

Humbly we pray that this mind
may be steadfast in us,
and that through these our hands,
and the hands of others
to whom thou shalt give the same spirit,
thou wilt vouchsafe to endow
the human family with new mercies.

- Francis Bacon—16th Century

May We Rise Through the Hardships

May we love ever more.
May we motivate ourselves to committed love in action.
May we motivate ourselves to live the life we wish to see in the
world.
May we be the transformation we wish to see in the world.
From the inside out . . .
From the roots branching upwards . . .
From the heart
to thought
to word
to action.
Through life's trials and hardships
we can arise beautiful and free.

- For Luna—Julia 'Butterfly' Hill, 2000

Infinite Peace to You

Deep peace of the running wave to you.
Deep peace of the flowing air to you.
Deep peace of the quiet earth to you.
Deep peace of the shining stars to you.
Deep peace of the infinite peace to you.

- Gaelic Blessing

You Will Go On

Tell yourself
as it gets cold and gray falls from the air
that you will go on
walking, hearing
the same tune no matter where...

And if it happens that you cannot
go on or turn back
and you find yourself
where you will be at the end,
tell yourself
in that final flowing of cold through your limbs
that you love what you are.

- Mark Strand

In Your Unbounded Mercy

We repent, O God most merciful, for all our sins;
for every thought that was false or unjust or unclean;
for every word spoken that ought not to have been spoken;
and for every deed done that ought not to have been done;

We repent for every deed and word and thought inspired by
selfishness,
and for every deed and word and thought inspired by hatred.
We repent most specially for every lustful thought and every lustful
action;
for every lie; for all hypocrisy;
for every promise given but not fulfilled,
and for all slander and backbiting.

Most specially also, we repent for every action
that has brought ruin to others,
for every word and deed that has given others pain;

In Your unbounded mercy, we ask you to forgive us, O God,
for all these sins committed by us,
and to forgive us for our constant failures
to think and speak and act according to Your will.

- Meher Baba, 1951

Walking with the Lord

Lord, take me where You want me to go;
Let me meet who You want me to meet;
Tell me what You want me to say; and
Keep me out of your way.

- Father Mechal Judge, FDNY—Died 9/11/01

Message for Loved Ones Left Behind

Do not stand at my grave and weep
I am not there; I do not sleep.
I am a thousand winds that blow,
I am the diamond glints on snow,
I am the sun on ripened grain,
I am the gentle autumn rain.
When you awaken in the morning's hush,
I am the swift uplifting rush
Of quiet birds in circled flight.
I am the soft stars that shine at night.
Do not stand at my grave and cry,
I am not there; I did not die.

- Mary Elizabeth Fry, 1932

Mother Teresa's Prayer for Purpose

Make us worthy, Lord, to serve our fellow men
throughout the world who live and die in poverty and hunger.

Give them through our hands this day their daily bread,
and by our understanding love, give peace and joy.

- Mother Teresa

Every Action is a Prayer

Pray to whoever you kneel down to:
Jesus nailed to his wooden or marble or plastic cross,
his suffering face bent to kiss you,
Buddha still under the Bo tree in scorching heat,
Adonai, Allah, raise your arms to Mary
that she may lay her palm on our brows,
Pray to the bus driver who takes you to work,
pray on the bus, pray for everyone riding that bus
and for everyone riding buses all over the world.
If you haven't been on a bus in a long time,
climb the few steps, drop some silver, and pray.

- Ellen Bass

Peace in the Heart

If there is to be peace in the world,
There must be peace in the nations.

If there is to be peace in the nations,
There must be peace in the cities.

If there is to be peace in the cities,
There must be peace between neighbors.

If there is to be peace between neighbors,
There must be peace in the home.

If there is to be peace in the home,
There must be peace in the heart.

- Lao Tzu

Forgiveness, Life and Love!

Violence never again!
War never again!
Terrorism never again!
In God's name,
may all religions bring upon earth
justice and peace,
forgiveness, life and love!

- Pope John Paul I, January 24, 2002

Give Thanks for This Day and Every Day

Creator, open our hearts
to peace and healing between all people.

Creator, open our hearts
to provide and protect for all children of the earth.

Creator, open our hearts
to respect for the earth, and all the gifts of the earth.

Creator, open our hearts
to end exclusion, violence, and fear among all.

Thank-you for the gifts of this day and every day.

- Native American Chant

You Can Always Hope

"Hope" is the thing with feathers
That perches in the soul.
And sings the tune without the words –
And never stops—at all.

And sweetest—in the Gale—is heard –
And sore must be the storm –
That could abash the little Bird
That kept so many warm.

I've heard it in the chillest land –
And on the strangest Sea –
Yet—never—in Extremity,
It asked a crumb—of me.

- Emily Dickinson

Life Is What Happens When

About suffering they were never wrong,
The Old Masters: how well they understood
Its human position; how it takes place
While someone else is eating or opening a window or just walking
dully along;
How, when the aged are reverently, passionately waiting
For the miraculous birth, there always must be
Children who did not specially want it to happen, skating
On a pond at the edge of the wood:
They never forgot
That even the dreadful martyrdom must run its course
Anyhow in a corner, some untidy spot
Where the dogs go on with their doggy life and the torturer's horse
Scratches its innocent behind on a tree.

- W.H. Auden, Musée Des Beaux Arts

Know That You Are Not Alone

All you who sleep tonight
Far from the ones you love,
No hand to left or right,
And emptiness above –

Know that you aren't alone.
The whole world shares your tears,
Some for two nights or one,
And some for all their years.

- Vikram Seth

May All Be At Peace

May I be filled with loving kindness.
May I be well.
May I be peaceful and at ease.
May I be happy.

- Tibetan Buddhist Meditation

June

The Shared Warmth of Love

"After every storm the sun will smile; for every problem there is a solution, and the soul's indefeasible duty is to be of good cheer."
—William R. Alger

"Rock bottom became the solid foundation on which I rebuilt my life."
—J.K. Rowling

"The best way to predict the future is to create it."
—Abraham Lincoln

"Why worry? If you've done the very best you can, worrying won't make it any better."
—Walt Disney

Thy Neighbor As Thyself

Let the warmth of the sun heal us
wherever we are broken.
Let it burn away the fog so that
we can see each other clearly.
So that we can see beyond labels,
beyond accents, gender or skin color.
Let the warmth and brightness
of the sun melt our selfishness.
So that we can share the joys and
feel the sorrows of our neighbors.
And let the light of the sun
be so strong that we will see all
people as our neighbors.
Let the earth, nourished by rain,
bring forth flowers
to surround us with beauty.
And let the mountains teach our hearts
to reach upward to heaven.

- Rabbi Harold Kushner

Recovery Poem

When my mother was in a hospital drying out,
or drinking at a pace that would put her there soon,
I would slip in the side door,

light an aromatic candle,
and bargain for us both.

- Robert Haas

When You Feel You Have Hit the Bottom

When I had nothing more to lose, I was given everything. When I ceased to be who I am, I found myself. When I experienced humiliation and yet kept on walking, I understood that I was free to choose my destiny.

- Paolo Coelho

Under God's Shelter

Oh Almighty! May he protect all of us!
May he cause us to enjoy!
May we acquire strength together.
May our knowledge become brilliant!
May we not hate each other! Oh Almighty!

May everybody be happy!
May all be free from ailments!
May we see what is auspicious!
May no one be subject to miseries!
Oh Almighty! May there be a Peace! Peace! Peace! Everywhere.

- Kathopanisada 2:6:19, India—1400 BC

The Ten Commandments for Cancer Survival

Thou shalt regard the word "Cancer" as exactly that: a word. Nothing more, nothing less. For its original meaning has changed mightily over the years, as have such words as Smallpox, TB, and Polio, all once dreaded ailments, now non-existent as maladies. And thus, too, shalt go thy Cancer. The answer shall come to those who shall be present to hear it. Be present to hear it when it comes.

Thou shalt love thy chemotherapy, thy radiation, and thy other treatments even as thyself, for they are thy friends and champions. Although they may exact a toll for their endeavors, they are oft most generous in the favors they bestow.

Thou shalt participate fully in thy recovery. Thou shalt learn all the details of thy ailment, its diagnosis, its prognosis, its treatments, conventional and alternative. Thou shalt discuss them openly and candidly with thy oncologist and shalt question all that thou dost not comprehend. Then, thou shalt cooperate intelligently and knowledgeably with thy doctor.

Thou shalt regard thy ailment as a temporary detour in thy life and shalt plan thy future as though this detour had not occurred. Thou shalt never, at no time, no how, regard thy temporary ailment as permanent. Thou shalt set long-term goals for thyself. For thou wilt verily recover, and your believing so will contribute mightily to thy recovery.

Thou shalt express thy feelings candidly and openly to thy loved ones, for they, too, are stricken. Thou shalt comfort and reassure them, for they, too, needest comforting and reassurance, even as thou dost.

Thou shalt be a comfort to thy fellow-cancerites, providing knowledge, encouragement, understanding and love. You shalt give them hope where there may be none, for only in hope lies their salvation. And by doing so, thou providest comfort for thyself, as well.

Thou shalt never relinquish hope, no matter how thou mayest feel at that moment, for thou knowest, in the deep recesses of thy heart, that your discouragement is but fleeting, and that a better day awaits thee, perhaps tomorrow, perhaps the day after tomorrow.

Thou shalt not regard thy ailment as the sum total of thy life but as merely a part of it. Fill your life with other diversions, be they mundane, daring, altruistic, or merely amusing. To fill your life with your ailment is to surrender to it.

Thou shalt maintain, at all times and in all circumstances, thy sense of humor, for laughter lightens thy heart and hastens thy recovery. This is not an easy task, sometimes seemingly impossible, but it is a goal well worth the Endeavour.

Thou shalt have enduring and unassailable faith, whether thy faith be in a Supreme Being, in Medical Science, in Thy Future, in Thyself, or in Whatever. Steadfastly sustain thy faith, for it shall sustain thee.

- Paul H. Klein

All Is Well

All is well

Death is nothing at all.
I have only slipped away into the next room.
I am I, and you are you.
Whatever we were to each other, that we still are.
Call me by my old familiar name,
speak to me in the easy way which you always used.
Put no difference in your tone,
wear no forced air of solemnity or sorrow.
Laugh as we always laughed at the little jokes we enjoyed together.
Pray, smile, think of me, pray for me.
Let my name be ever the household word that it always was,
let it be spoken without effect,
without the trace of a shadow on it.
Life means all that it ever meant.
It is the same as it ever was;
there is unbroken continuity.
Why should I be out of mind because I am out of sight?
I am waiting for you,
for an interval,
somewhere very near,
just round the corner.
All is well.

- Henry Scott Holland 1847-1918
Canon of St. Paul's Cathedral

Where There is Despair, Hope

Lord, make me an instrument of Thy peace;
where there is hatred, let me sow love;
where there is injury, pardon;
where there is doubt, faith;
where there is despair, hope;
where there is darkness, light;
and where there is sadness, joy.

O Divine Master,
grant that I may not so much seek

to be consoled as to console;
to be understood, as to understand;
to be loved, as to love;
for it is in giving that we receive,
it is in pardoning that we are pardoned,
and it is in dying that we are born to eternal life.

Amen..

- St. Francis of Assisi

One Hour In Thy Hands

The shadow of my finger cast
Divides the future from the past:
Before it, sleeps the unborn hour
In darkness, and beyond thy power:

Behind its unreturning line,
The vanished hour, no longer thine:
One hour alone is in thy hands, –
The NOW on which the shadow stands.

- Henry Van Dyke, 1904;
The Sun Dial at Wells College

God Unrolls the Canvas

My life is but a weaving

Between my Lord and me;
I cannot choose the colors

He weaveth steadily.

Oft' times He weaveth sorrow
And I, in foolish pride
forget He sees the upper
And I the underside.

Not till the loom is silent
And the shuttles cease to fly
Shall God unroll the canvas
And explain the reason why.

The dark threads are as needful
In the weaver's skillful hand
As the threads of gold and silver
In the pattern He has planned.

He knows, He loves, He cares;
Nothing this truth can dim.
He gives the very best to those
Who leave the choice with Him.

- Corrie ten Boom

Going Home

I believe there is Someone waiting for me, Waiting to say:
"Welcome Home !"

Someone I have never seen, but whom I will recognize in the
depths of my heart
because He has lived there since the beginning of time.

Someone who has never doubted my return,
never failed to still my doubts about my return.

I believe there is Someone who knows me so intimately,
loves me so totally, that joy will spark spontaneously
when we reunite in the land of immortal Birth.
Tears will be wiped away;
Sadness and fear will disappear as mist when it meets the morning
sun.
This is whom I seek, seeks me.
He has never left me alone.
For He is Self of myself,

Soul of my soul,
Life of my very life.

- Sister Joan Metzner

Every Tomorrow is a Vision of Hope

Look to this day,

For yesterday is but a dream,
And tomorrow is only a vision,
But today, well lived,
Makes every yesterday a dream of happiness,
And every tomorrow a vision of hope.
Look well, therefore, to this day.

- Kalidasa, from ancient Sanskrit

Love

is giving with no thought of getting. It is tenderness enfolding with
strength to protect. It is forgiveness without further thought of
the thing forgiven. It is understanding of human weakness, with
knowledge of the true man shining through. It is quiet in the midst
of turmoil. It is trust in God with no thought of self. It is the one
altogether lovely, the light in the mother's eyes, the glory in the
sacrifice, the quiet assurance of protection.

It is in the expectation of our Father's promise coming true. It is the refusal to see anything but good in our fellow man. It is the glory that comes with selflessness and the power that comes with assurance of the Father's love for His Children. It is the voice that says "no" to our brother, though "yes" might be more easily said. It is resistance to the world's lust and greed, thus becoming a positive law of annihilation to error.

Love...the one thing no one can take from us...the one thing we can give constantly and become increasingly rich in the giving. Love can take no offence, for it cannot know that which it does not of itself conceive. It cannot hurt or be hurt, for it is the purest reflection of GOD, Good. It is the one eternal, indestructible force for Good. It is the will of GOD, preparing, planning, proposing always what is best for all His universe.

- S. Miriam Clifford;
Broken But Not Destroyed: In Search for God

Time Stands Still For Those Who Love

Hours fly, flowers die.
New days, new ways, pass by!
Love stays.

Time is

Too slow for those who wait,

Too swift for those who fear,
Too long for those who grieve,

Too short for those who rejoice,
But for those who love,
Time is not.

- Henry Van Dyke; Inscription for Katrina's Sundial

Accept Tomorrow with a Happy Heart

Let each day be so fashioned as though
it were closing the line of days
and completely fulfilling life.

If then God grants us the morrow,
let us accept it with a happy heart.

- Seneca

His Eye Watches Over Me

I arise today
Through a mighty strength:

God's power to guide me,
God's might to uphold me,
God's eyes to watch over me;
God's ear to hear me,

God's word to give me speech,
God's hand to guard me,
God's way to lie before me,
God's shield to shelter me,
God's host to secure me.

- St. Brigid

Desiderata

Go placidly amid the noise and haste,
and remember what peace there may be in silence.
As far as possible without surrender
be on good terms with all persons.
Speak your truth quietly and clearly;
and listen to others,
even the dull and the ignorant;
they too have their story.

Avoid loud and aggressive persons,
they are vexations to the spirit.
If you compare yourself with others,
you may become vain and bitter;
for always there will be greater and lesser persons than yourself.
Enjoy your achievements as well as your plans.

Keep interested in your own career, however humble;

it is a real possession in the changing fortunes of time.
Exercise caution in your business affairs;

for the world is full of trickery.
But let this not blind you to what virtue there is;
many persons strive for high ideals;
and everywhere life is full of heroism. Be yourself.
Especially, do not feign affection.
Neither be cynical about love;
for in the face of all aridity and disenchantment
it is as perennial as the grass.

Take kindly the counsel of the years,
gracefully surrendering the things of youth.
Nurture strength of spirit to shield you in sudden misfortune.
But do not distress yourself with dark imaginings.
Many fears are born of fatigue and loneliness.
Beyond a wholesome discipline,
be gentle with yourself.

You are a child of the universe,
no less than the trees and the stars;
you have a right to be here.
And whether or not it is clear to you,
no doubt the universe is unfolding as it should.

Therefore be at peace with God,
whatever you conceive Him to be,
and whatever your labors and aspirations,
in the noisy confusion of life keep peace with your soul.

With all its sham, drudgery, and broken dreams,
it is still a beautiful world.

Be cheerful.
Strive to be happy.

- Max Ehrmann, 1927

Compassion for the Dying

Our attitude to all men would be Christian if we regarded them as though they were dying and determined our relation to them in the light of death, both of their death and our own.

A person who is dying calls for a special kind of feeling. Our attitude to him is at once softened and lifted onto a higher plane. We can then feel compassion for people whom we do not love. But every man is dying, I too am dying and must never forget about death.

- Nikolai Berdyaev

I Love You

Not only for what you are,
but for what I am when I'm with you,
I Love You
For the part of me that you bring out,
I Love You
For putting your hand into my heaped-up heart
and passing over all the foolish, weak things
that you can't help dimly seeing there,

and for drawing out into the light
all the beautiful belongings that no one else
had looked quite far enough to find.

I Love You
because you are helping me to
make of the lumber of my life not a tavern but a temple;
out of the works of my every day not a reproach,
but a song....

- Anonymous

Live As If Today Is Your Last

Ah, Fill the cup –

What boots it to repeat

How time is slipping underneath our feet,
Unborn Tomorrow,
And dead Yesterday
Why fret about them

If Today be sweet!!

- Omar Khayyam

We Can Be Kind

So many things we can't control
So many hurts that happen every day
So many heartaches that pierce the soul
So much pain that won't ever go away
How do we make it better?
How do we make it through?
What can we do when there's nothing we can do?

We can be Kind
We can take care of each other
We can remember that deep down inside we all need the same
thing
And maybe we'll find
If we are there for each other
That together we'll weather whatever tomorrow may bring
Nobody really wants to fight
Nobody really wants to go to war

Everyone wants to make things right
So what are we always fighting for?
Does nobody want to see it?
Does nobody understand?
The power to heal is right here in our hand.

We can be Kind
We can take care of each other
We can remember that deep down inside we all need the same
thing
And maybe we'll find

If we are there for each other
That together we'll weather whatever tomorrow may bring

- David Friedman

There is a Love That Never Fails

There is an Eye that never sleeps,
beneath the wind of night.
There is an Ear that never shuts,
When sinks the beam of light.
There is an Arm that never tires,
When human strength gives way.
There is a Love that never fails,
When earthly loves decay.

- George Mathewson

Miracle Prayer for Financial Troubles

Heavenly Father, You are my rock and my fortress. It is within You I find the answer to my every need. I praise You for You are the one who moves mountains and walks on water.

I believe with all my heart and soul that You can calm the rough seas of debt in my life. You desire to be my ever-present help in times of trouble, all kinds, even in the depths of financial dispair. You are aware of every part of my financial situation. You see my material needs today. You see my lack of money and my debt.

Lord, you see my mind and emotions filled with the heavy burdens of unpaid bills, and the struggles I am facing. Heavenly Father, you see it all. Nothing has escaped your gaze, and I know You are watching over me. I come to You asking for You to bring Your loving intervention into my finances. Show me how to get out of every financial struggle in my life. Teach me how to bring my finances into a healthy place. Guide me in each financial decision that I make today, tomorrow, and always. Give me a vision of debt-free living that will motivate me, and propel me to that blessed place of financial peace that I know is possible. Father, thank you for every good gift You give to me. Amen..

- Chapel of the Holy Land

Persist

When things go wrong, as they sometimes will,
When the road you're trudging seems all up hill,
When the funds are low and the debts are high,
And you want to smile, but you have to sigh,
When care is pressing you down a bit,
Rest, if you must—but don't you quit.
Life is queer with its twists and turns,
As every one of us sometimes learns,
And many a failure turns about,
When he might have won had he stuck it out,
Don't give up, though the pace seems slow...
You might succeed with another blow.
Often the goal is nearer than

It seems to a faint and faltering man.
Often the struggler has given up,
When he might have captured the victor's cup,
And he learned too late, when the night slipped down,
How close he was to the golden crown.
Success is failure turned inside out,
The silver tint to the clouds of doubt –
And you can never tell how close you are,
It may appear when it seems afar;
So stick to the fight when you're hardest hit –
It's when things seem worst that you mustn't quit!

- Anonymous

Reading the Book of Life

Everything that happens
And everything that befalls us has a meaning,
But it is often difficult to recognize it.
Also in the book of life every page has two sides:
We human beings fill the upper side with our plans, hopes, and
wishes,
But Providence writes on the other side,
And what it ordains is seldom our goal.

- Nisami

To Those I Love

If I should ever leave you
To go along the silent way, grieve not,
Nor speak of me with tears, but laugh and talk
Of me as if I were beside you there.
(I'd come—I'd come, could I but find a way!
But would not tears and grief be barriers?)
And when you hear a song or see a bird
I loved, please do not let the thought of me
Be sad... for I am loving you just as I always have.
You were so good to me!
There are so many things I wanted still
To do—so many things to say to you.
Remember that I did not fear. It was
Just leaving you that was so hard to face.
We cannot see beyond. But this I know:
I loved you so—`twas heaven here with you!

- Isla Paschal Richardson

Truth and Beauty

A thing of beauty is a joy forever;
Its loveliness increases;
It will never pass into nothingness;
But still will keep
A bower quiet for us, and a sleep

Full of sweet dreams, and health,
And quiet breathing.

- John Keats

The Big Questions of Life

The question
for each man to settle
is not what he would do if he had
means, time, influence, and educational advantages,
but what he will do with the things he has.

- Hamilton Wright Mabie

A Heart Illumined

My shortest days end,
My lengthening days begin.
What matters more or less sun in the sky,
When all is sun within?

- Christina G. Rossetti

Live Each Day As If It Is Your Last

As my life today
has been determined by the way I lived my yesterday,
So my tomorrow is being determined by the way I live my today.

- Ralph Waldo Trine

When Your Heart Is Broken Open

Tragedy always brings about radical change in our lives, a change
that is associated with the same principle: loss. When faced by any
loss, there's no point in trying to recover what has been; it's best to
take advantage of the large space that opens up before us and fill it
with something new.

- Paulo Coelho, Aleph

July

The Bounty and Beauty of This World

"Tough times never last, but tough people do."
—Robert H. Schuller

"Use what you've been through as fuel, believe in yourself."
—Yvonne Pierre

"When everything seems to be going against you, remember that the airplane takes off against the wind, not with it."
—Henry Ford

"The gem cannot be polished without friction, nor man perfected without trials."
—Chinese Proverb

Face Your Fears and Find the Meaning of Your Life

The cave you fear to enter holds the treasure that you seek.

- Joseph Campbell

Through Him All Things Are Possible

O heavenly Father, you have filled the world with beauty: Open our
eyes to behold your gracious hand in all your works; that, rejoicing
in your whole creation, we may learn to serve you with gladness;
for the sake of him through whom all things were made, your Son
Jesus Christ our Lord. Amen..

- The Book of Common Prayer

Though I May Stumble, I Will Not Fall

As the rain hides the stars,
as the autumn mist
hides the hills,
as the clouds veil
the blue of the sky, so
the dark happenings of my lot
hide the shining of thy face from me.
Yet, if I may hold thy hand in the darkness,
it is enough, since I know,

that though I may stumble in my going,
Thou dost not fall.

- Ancient Scottish Song

Enfold Me In Your Protective Arms

Circle me, Lord.
Keep protection near
And danger afar.

Circle me, Lord
Keep hope within.
Keep doubt without.

Circle me, Lord.
Keep light near
And darkness afar.

Circle me, Lord.
Keep peace within.
Keep evil out.

- Irish Blessing

Enough For All

Ground of all being,
Source of all life, Father of the universe,
Your name is sacred, beyond speaking.

May we know your presence,
may your longings be our longings in heart and in action.
May there be food for the human family today
and for the whole earth community.

Forgive us the falseness of what we have done
as we forgive those who are untrue to us.

Do not forsake us in our time of conflict
but lead us into new beginnings.

For the light of life, the vitality of life,
and the glory of life are yours, now and forever.

Amen..

- *The Casa Del Sol Prayer of Jesus*

Connected Through the Web of Life

I am the wind on the sea
I am the ocean wave
I am the sound of the billows.
I am the seven-horned stag
I am the hawk on the cliff

I am the dewdrop in sunlight
I am the fairest of flowers
I am the raging boar
I am the salmon in the deep pool
I am the lake on the plain
I am the meaning of the poem
I am the point of the spear
I am the god who makes fire in the head
Who levels the mountain?
Who speaks the age of the moon?
Who has been where the sun sleeps?
Who, if not I?

- Ancient Celtic Invocation; The Song of Amergin

Justice, God, and All Goodness

Grant, O God, thy protection,
and in protection, strength,
and in strength, understanding,
and in understanding, knowledge,
and in knowledge, the knowledge of justice,
and in the knowledge of justice, the love of it,
and in that love, the love of all existences,
and in the love of all existences, the love of God,
God and all goodness.

- Gorsedd Prayer, 1792

Someone to Watch Over You

As you leave this place
may the Living Lord go with you;
May he go behind you, to encourage you,
beside you, to befriend you,
above you, to watch over you,
beneath you, to lift you from your sorrows,
within you, to give you the gifts of faith, hope, and love,
and always before you, to show you the way.

- Benediction

When the World Is Too Much With Us

On the day when
the weight deadens
on your shoulders
and you stumble,
may the clay dance
to balance you.
And when your eyes
freeze behind
the grey window
and the ghost of loss
gets in to you,
may a flock of colors,
indigo, red, green,
and azure blue

come to awaken in you
a meadow of delight.

- Anonymous; 1934

Showering Gifts Upon Thee

We bathe your palms
In the showers of wine,
In the crook of the kindling,
In the seven elements,
In the sap of the tree,
In the milk of honey;

We place nine pure, choice gifts
In your clear beloved face:

The gift of form,
The gift of voice,
The gift of fortune,
The gift of goodness,
The gift of eminence,
The gift of charity,
The gift of integrity,
The gift of true nobility,
The gift of apt speech.

- Traditional Gaelic Blessing

A Psalm of David: The Lord is My Shepherd

The Lord is my shepherd, I shall not want.
He makes me lie down in green pastures;
He leads me beside still waters;
He restores my soul.
He leads me in right paths
for His name's sake.

Even though I walk through the darkest valley,
I fear no evil;
for You are with me;
Your rod and Your staff –
they comfort me.

You prepare a table before me
in the presence of my enemies;
You anoint my head with oil;
my cup overflows.
Surely goodness and mercy shall follow me
all the days of my life,
and I shall dwell in the house of the Lord
my whole life long.

- Psalm 23, ESV

Let Me Walk In Beauty Beside You

O Great Spirit,
whose voice I hear in the winds,

---

and whose breath gives life to all the world
–hear me–
I come before you, one of your children.
I am small and weak.
I need your strength and wisdom.
Let me walk in beauty and make my eyes ever behold
the red and purple sunset.
Make my hands respect the things you have made,
my ears sharp to hear your voice.
Make me wise, so that I may know the things
you have taught my People.
The lessons you have hidden in every leaf and rock.
I seek strength not to be superior to my brothers,
but to be able to fight my greatest enemy,
myself.
Make me ever ready to come to you,
with clean hands and straight eyes,
so when life fades as a fading sunset,
my spirit may come to you without shame.

- *Traditional Native American Prayer*

Happiness is the Way

You should be happy right in the here and now.
There is no way to enlightenment.
Enlightenment should be right here and right now.
The moment when you come back to yourself,

mind and body together,
fully present, fully alive,

that is already enlightenment...
You are fully alive.
You are awake.
Enlightenment is there.

And if you continue each moment like that,
enlightenment becomes deeper.

- Thich Nhat Hanh

Think Only of Today and Take Comfort In Tomorrow

Do not look forward to what might happen tomorrow. The same everlasting Father who cared for you today will care for you tomorrow and every day. Either he will shield you from suffering or he will give you unfailing strength to bear it. Be at peace, then, and put aside all anxious thoughts and imaginations.

- St. Francis de Sales

Relief in Times of Distress

Answer me when I call to you, O my righteous God.
Give me relief from my distress; be merciful to me and hear
my prayer.

Many are asking, "Who can show us any good?"
Let the light of your face shine upon us, O Lord.
You have filled my heart with greater joy
than when their grain and new wine abound.
I will lie down and sleep in peace,
for you alone, O Lord, make me dwell in safety.

- Psalm 4:1, 6-8, NIV

Prayer for Peaceful Sleep

Oh Righteous God,
Bring relief from the pain and suffering of my life.
Help us to look to you to show us good in the midst of bad.
Let your face shine on us.

Bring hope and joy to my heart once again.
Allow my sleep to once again be peaceful.
Let me dwell with you in safety.

Amen..

- Author Unknown

Counting Our Blessings Every Day

For the expanding grandeur of creation, worlds known and
unknown, galaxies beyond galaxies, filling us with awe and

challenging our imaginations:
We give thanks this day.

For this fragile planet earth,
its times and tides, its sunsets and seasons:
We give thanks this day.

For the joy of human life,
its wonders and surprises, its hopes and achievements:
We give thanks this day.

For high hopes and noble causes, for faith without fanaticism, for
understanding of views not shared:
We give thanks this day.

For all who have labored and suffered for a fairer world, who have
lived so that others might live in dignity and freedom:
We give thanks this day.

For human liberty and sacred rites; for opportunities to change
and grow, to affirm and choose:
We give thanks this day.

We pray that we may live not by our fears but by our hopes, not by
our words but by our deeds.
We give thanks this day.

- O. Eugene Pickett

We Are Reborn

O Holy Child of Bethlehem,
descend to us, we pray;
Cast out our sin, and enter in,
be born in us today.

- Phillips Brooks, 1867

Each Day Is A Gift

I didn't expect to recover from my second operation, but since I did, I consider that I'm living on borrowed time. Every day that dawns is a gift to me, and I take it that way. I accept it gratefully without looking beyond it. I completely forget my physical suffering and all the unpleasantness of my present condition and I think only of the joy of seeing the sun rise once more and of being able to work a little bit, even under difficult conditions.

- Henri Matisse

Buddhist Blessing: Auspicious Wish

At this very moment, for the peoples and the nations of the earth,
May not even the names disease, war, famine, and suffering be heard.
Rather may their moral conduct, merit, wealth, and prosperity

increase,
and may good fortune and well-being always arise for them.

- Kyabje Dudjom Rinpoche

Give Love, Peace and Joy

Make us worthy, Lord, to serve our fellow men
throughout the world who live and die in poverty and hunger.

Give them through our hands this day their daily bread,
and by our understanding love, give peace and joy.

- Mother Teresa

Arise in Radiance

The earth is full of your goodness,
your greatness and understanding,
your wisdom and harmony.
How wonderful are the lights that you created.
You formed them with strength and power
and they shine very wonderfully on the world,
magnificent in their splendor.
They arise in radiance and go down in joy.
Reverently they fulfill your divine will.

And treasure for me every grace.
At the Offertory time
Please offer me to God Divine.
All I have and all I am,
Present it with the Precious Lamb.
Adore for me the great Oblation.
Pray for all I hold most dear
Be they far or be they near.
Rmember, too, my own dear dead
For whom Christ's Precious Blood was shed.
And at Communion bring to me
Christ's Flesh and Blood, my food to be.
To give me strength and holy grace
A pledge to see Him face to face
And when the Holy Mass is done
Then with His blessing, come back home.

- Sisters of His Holy Name

You Never Walk Alone

Wherever I go, only Thou!
Wherever I stand, only Thou!
Just Thou, again Thou!
Always Thou!
Thou, Thou, Thou!
When things are good, Thou!

When things are bad, Thou!
Thou, Thou, Thou!

- Hasidic Ode

Walking the Beautiful Trail

With your feet I walk
I walk with your limbs
I carry forth your body
For me your mind thinks
Your voice speaks for me
Beauty is before me
And beauty is behind me
Above and below me hovers the beautiful
I am surrounded by it
I am immersed in it
In my youth I am aware of it
And in old age I shall walk quietly
The beautiful trail.

- Navajo Song

When Storms of Sorrow Toss My Soul

When once I mourned a load of sin,
When conscience felt a wound within,
When all my works were thrown away,

When on my knees I knelt to pray,
Then, blissful hour, remembered well,
I learned Thy love, Immanuel!

When storms of sorrow toss my soul,
When waves of care around me roll,
When comforts sink, when joys shall flee,
When hopeless griefs shall gape for me,
One word the tempest's rage shall quell,
That word, Thy name, Immanuel !

When for the truth I suffer shame,
When foes pour scandal on my name,
When cruel taunts and jeers abound,
When "bulls of Bashan" gird me round,
Secure within my tower I'll dwell,
That tower, Thy grace, Immanuel!

When hell, enraged, lifts up her roar,
When Satan stops my path before,
When fiends rejoice, and wait my end,
When legion'd hosts their arrows send,
Fear not, my soul, but hurl at hell
Thy battle-cry, Immanuel!

When down the hill of life I go,

When o'er my feet death's waters flow,
When in the deep'ning flood I sink,
When friends stand weeping on the brink,

I'll mingle with my last farewell,
Thy lovely name, Immanuel!

When tears are banished from mine eye,
When fairer worlds than these are nigh,
When Heaven shall fill my ravish'd sight,
When I shall bathe in sweet delight,
One joy all joys shall far excel,
To see Thy face, Immanuel!

- Charles Spurgeon, 1853

The Gateway to All Understanding

The Tao that can be told
is not the eternal Tao.

The name that can be named
is not the eternal Name.

The unnamable is the eternally real.

Naming is the origin
of all particular things.

Free from desire, you realize the mystery.

Caught in desire, you see only the manifestations.

Yet mystery and manifestations
arise from the same source.

This source is called darkness.

Darkness within darkness.

The gateway to all understanding.

- Tao Te Ching

Before Heaven and Earth

Empty of all doctrines,
The Tao is wisdom eternally inexhaustible.

Fathomless for the mere intellect,
The Tao is the law wherewith all things come into being.

It blunts the edges of the intellect,
Untangles the knots of the mind,
Softens the glare of thinking,
And settles the dust of thought.

Transparent yet invisible,
The Tao exists like deep pellucid water.

Its origin is unknown,
For it existed before Heaven and Earth

- Lao Tzu, 600 BC

August

Shining Your Light for All to See

"Never let your head hang down. Never give up and sit down and grieve. Find another way. And don't pray when it rains if you don't pray when the sun shines."
—Leroy Satchel Paige

"The difference between stumbling blocks and stepping stones is how you use them."
—Unknown

"In normal life we hardly realize how much more we receive than we give, and life cannot be rich without such gratitude."
—Dietrich Bonhoeffer

"The unthankful heart discovers no mercies, but the thankful heart will find, in every hour, some heavenly blessings."
—Henry Ward Beecher

Give Us This Day

Finish each day and be done with it.

You have done what you could.

Some blunders and absurdities no doubt crept in;
forget them as soon as you can.

Tomorrow is a new day; begin it serenely
and with too high a spirit to be encumbered by your old nonsense.

- Ralph Waldo Emerson

Don't Just Go Through It, Grow Through It

An attitude of gratitude can make a profound difference in our
day-to-day lives, yet as we all come to know, not every day is filled
with good things. We each endure difficult passages: illnesses,
money trouble, work woes, relationship issues, the loss of a
loved one, and countless others. These are the vicissitudes of life.
However, it is the attitude you bring to each situation that makes
all the difference. Share what you learned from others through
your life lessons and offer it if you think it can be of help to a fellow
traveler who is walking a hard path.

- Brenda Knight

Awaken My Heart

Holy Spirit,

Giving life to all life,

Moving all creatures,

Root of all things,

Washing them clean,

Wiping out their mistakes,

Healing their wounds,

You are our true life,

Luminous, wonderful,

Awakening the heart from its ancient sleep.

- Hildegarde of Bingen, 1140

Original Lord's Prayer

Release a space to plant your Presence here.

Envision your "I Can" now.

Embody your desire in every light and form.

Grow through us this moment's bread and wisdom.

Untie the knots of failure binding us,
as we release the strands we hold of others' faults.

Help us not forget our Source,
Yet free us from not being in the Present.

From you arises every Vision, Power and Song
from gathering to gathering.

Amen. –

May our future actions grow from here!

- Translated from the Original Aramaic

Lord, Take the Wheel

Steersman unseen! henceforth the helms are Thine;

Take Thou command—(what to my petty skill Thy navigation?).

My hands, my limbs grow nerveless;
My brain feels rack'd, bewilder'd;

Let the old timbers part—I will not part!

I will cling fast to Thee, O God, though the waves buffet me;
Thee, Thee at least, I know.

- Walt Whitman

All Miracles Are Possible

Bless Thee, O Lord,
for the living arc of the sky over me this morning.

Bless Thee, O Lord,
for the companionship of night mist
far above the skyscraper peaks I saw
when I woke once during the night.

Bless Thee, O Lord,
for the miracle of light to my eyes
and the mystery of it ever changing.

Bless Thee, O Lord,
for the laws Thou hast ordained holding fast
these tall oblongs of stone and steel,
holding fast the planet Earth in its course
and farther beyond the circle of the Sun.

- Carl Sandburg

His Word is Who We Are

image of God
born of God's breath
vessel of divine Love
after his likeness
dwelling of God
capacity for the infinite

eternally known
chosen of God
home of the Infinite Majesty
abiding in the Son
called from eternity
life in the Lord
temple of the Holy Spirit
branch of Christ
receptacle of the Most High
wellspring of Living Water
heir of the kingdom
the glory of God
abode of the Trinity.

God sings this litany
eternally in his Word.

This is who you are.

- Trappist Monk Litany

Keep Looking for Those Silver Linings

If you want the rainbow, you have to put up with the rain.

- Dolly Parton

Safe In Your Hands

Father, I abandon myself into your hands;
do with me what you will.

Whatever you may do, I thank you:
I am ready for all, I accept all.

Let only your will be done in me,
and in all Your creatures –

I wish no more than this, O Lord.

Into your hands I commend my soul;
I offer it to you with all the love of my heart,
for I love you, Lord,
and so need to give myself,
to surrender myself into your hands,
without reserve,
and with boundless confidence,
For you are my Father.

- Charles de Foucault

The Garden of Heaven

Saint Therese, the little flower

Please pick me

A rose from the heavenly garden

And send it to me

With a message of love.

Ask God to grant me

The favor I thee implore

And tell him I will love him

Each day more and more.

- Petition to St. Therese of Lisieux

I Will Not Fear, For You Are Ever With Me

My Lord God,

I have no idea where I am going

I do not see the road ahead of me.

I cannot know for certain where it will end.

Nor do I really know myself,
And the fact that I think I am following
your will does not mean that I am
actually doing so.

But I believe that the desire to please
you does in fact please you.

And I hope that I have that desire in all
that I am doing.

And I know that if I do this, you
will lead me by the right road
though I may know nothing about it.

Therefore I will trust you always
though I may seem to be lost
and in the shadow of death, I will
not fear, for you are ever with me
and you will never leave me
to face my perils alone.

- Thomas Merton

Shelter Me

Soul of Christ, sanctify me;
Body of Christ, save me;
Blood of Christ, inebriate me;
Water from the side of Christ, wash me;
Passion of Christ, strengthen me;
O good Jesus, hear me;
Within Thy wounds, hide me;
Permit me not to be separated from 'Thee;
From the wicked foe defend me;
In the hour of my death call me,
And bid me come unto Thee,

That with all Thy saints I may praise Thee
For ever and ever.

Amen..

- Saint Ignatius Loyola, 16th Century

The Prayer of Jabez

Oh, that You would bless me indeed,
and enlarge my territory,
that Your hand would be with me,
and that You would keep me from evil,
that I may be free from pain!

- 1 Chronicles 4:10, NIV

Kindness Everlasting

O praise the Lord,
all ye nations;
praise him, all ye people.

For his merciful kindness is great toward us;
and the truth of the Lord endureth for ever.

Praise ye the Lord.

- Psalm 117:1, KJV

Keep Praying, No Matter What

Pray inwardly, even if you do not enjoy it.

It does good, though you feel nothing.

Yes, even though you think you are doing nothing.

Prayer is not overcoming God's reluctance.

It is laying hold of His willingness.

This is our Lord's will, ...that our prayer and our trust be
alike large.

For if we do not trust as much as we pray,
we fail in full worship to our Lord in our prayer;
and also we hinder and hurt ourselves.

The reason is that we do not know truly
that our Lord is the ground from which our prayer springeth;
nor do we know that it is given us by his grace and his love.

If we knew this, it would make us trust
to have of our Lord's gifts all that we desire.

For I am sure that no man asketh mercy and grace with sincerity,
without mercy and grace being given to him first.

- Julian of Norwich, 1373

Take Away My Difficulties

God, I offer myself to Thee –
to build with me
and to do with me as Thou wilt.

Relieve me of the bondage of self,
that I may better do Thy will.

Take away my difficulties,
that victory over them may bear witness
to those I would help of Thy Power,
Thy Love, and Thy Way of life.

May I do Thy will always!

- Alcoholics Anonymous Big Book, 1939

Let Me Do Your Will

I am no longer my own, but thine.

Put me to what thou wilt, rank me with whom thou wilt.

Put me to doing, put me to suffering.

Let me be employed for thee or laid aside for thee,
exalted for thee or brought low for thee.

Let me be full, let me be empty.

Let me have all things, let me have nothing.

I freely and heartily yield all things to thy pleasure and disposal.

And now, O glorious and blessed God, Father, Son and Holy Spirit,
thou art mine, and I am thine.

So be it.

And the covenant which I have made on earth,
let it be ratified in heaven.

Amen..

- John Wesley, 1755

Love Lifts Us Up

In this life we cannot do great things.

We can only do small things with great love.

- Mother Teresa

The Imagination of the Heart

My soul doth magnify the Lord,
And my spirit hath rejoiced in God my Savior.

For he hath regarded
the low estate of his handmaiden:

for, behold, from henceforth
all generations shall call me blessed.

For he that is mighty hath done to me great things;
and holy is his name.

And his mercy is on them that fear him
from generation to generation.

He hath shewed strength with his arm;
he hath scattered the proud in the imagination of their hearts.

He hath put down the mighty from their seats,
and hath exalted them of low degree.

He hath filled the hungry with good things;
and the rich he hath sent empty away.

He hath holpen his servant Israel,
in remembrance of his mercy;
As he spake to our fathers, to Abraham,
and to his seed for ever.

Magnificat anima mea Dominum

Et exultavit spiritus meus in Deo salutari meo.

Quia respexit humilitatem ancillæ suæ:

ecce enim ex hoc beatam me dicent omnes generationes.

Quia fecit mihi magna qui potens est, et sanctum nomen eius.

Et misericordia eius a progenie in progenies timentibus eum.

Fecit potentiam in bracchio suo, dispersit superbos mente cordi sui

Deposuit potentes de sede et exaltavit humiles.

Esurientes implevit bonis et divites dimisit inanes,

Suscepit Israel puerum suum recordatus misericordiæ suæ,

Sicut locutus est ad patres nostros, Abraham et semini eius
in sæcula.

- *Song of Mary, Gospel of Luke 1:46-55, KJV*

Always Serene

Hail, Mary, White Lily of the Glorious and always-serene Trinity.

Hail brilliant Rose of the Garden of heavenly delights;

O you, by whom God wanted to be born and by whose milk

the King of Heaven wanted to be nourished!

Nourish our souls with effusions of divine grace.

Amen.!

- *Saint Gertrude*

Rejoice and Do Righteousness

For since the beginning of the world
Men have not heard nor perceived by the ear,
Nor has the eye seen any God besides You,
Who acts for the one who waits for Him.

You meet him who rejoices and does righteousness,
Who remembers You in Your ways.
You are indeed angry, for we have sinned –
In these ways we continue; and we need to be saved.

But we are all like an unclean thing,
And all our righteousnesses are like filthy rags;
We all fade as a leaf,
And our iniquities, like the wind, have taken us away.

And there is no one who calls on Your name,
Who stirs himself up to take hold of You;
For You have hidden Your face from us,
And have consumed us because of our iniquities.

But now, O Lord, You are our Father;
We are the clay, and You our potter;
And all we are the work of Your hand.

Do not be furious, O Lord,
Nor remember iniquity forever;
Indeed, please look—we all are Your people!

- Isaiah 64:4-9, KJV

After the Loss of a Pregnancy

O God, who gathered Rachel's tears over her lost children, hear now my/our sorrow and distress at the death of my/our expected child; in the darkness of loss, stretch out to me/us the strength of your arm and renewed assurance of your love; through your own suffering and your risen Child Jesus. Amen..

- Grace Cathedral

Trust In Him

Prayer is not asking.

Prayer is putting oneself in the hands of God,
at his disposition,
and listening to his voice in the depths of our hearts.

- Mother Teresa

Give Thanks Each and Every Day

To our Gods of old, we bless the ground
that you tread in search of our freedom!

We bless your presence in our lives and in our hearts!

Take of this offering to your delight,
and be filled with our prayers of thanksgiving!

May our lives remain as full as our hearts on this day!

- Yoruban Grace

The Migrant's Prayer

The journey towards you Lord, is life.

To set off, is to die a little.

To arrive is never to arrive, until one is at rest with you.

You, Lord, experienced migration.

You brought it upon all men who know what it is to live;
who seek safe passage to the gates of heaven.

You drove Abraham from his land, father of all believers.

You shall remember the paths leading to you, the prophets and
the apostles.

You yourself became a migrant from heaven to earth.

- Anonymous

Rise to the Level of Love

Another way that you love your enemy is this:

When the opportunity presents itself for you to defeat your enemy,
that is the time which you must not do it.
There will come a time, in many instances,
when the person who hates you most,
the person who has misused you most,
the person who has gossiped about you most,
the person who has spread false rumors about you most,
there will come a time when
you will have an opportunity to defeat that person.

It might be in terms of a recommendation for a job;
it might be in terms of helping that person
to make some move in life.

That's the time you must do it.

That is the meaning of love.

In the final analysis,
love is not this sentimental something that we talk about.

It's not merely an emotional something.

Love is creative, understanding goodwill for all men.

It is the refusal to defeat any individual.

When you rise to the level of love, of its great beauty and power,
you seek only to defeat evil systems.

Individuals who happen to be caught up in that system, you love,
but you seek to defeat the system.

- Dr. Martin Luther King, Jr., 1957

Grace and Gladness

Make a joyful noise unto the Lord, all ye lands.

Serve the Lord with gladness;
come before his presence with singing.

Know ye that the Lord he is God;
it is he that hath made us, and not we ourselves;
we are his people, and the sheep of his pasture.

Enter into his gates with thanksgiving,
and into his courts with praise;
be thankful unto him, and bless his name.

For the Lord is good; his mercy is everlasting;
and his truth endureth to all generations.

- Psalm 100, KJV

Difficulties Can Bring More Blessings

Blessed are they who give
without expecting even thanks in return,
for they shall be abundantly rewarded.

Blessed are they who love and trust their fellow beings,
for they shall reach the good in people and
receive a loving response.

Blessed are they who after dedicating their lives
and thereby receiving a blessing, have the courage and faith
to surmount the difficulties of the path ahead,
for they shall receive a second blessing.

Blessed are they who advance toward the spiritual path
without the selfish motive of seeking inner peace,

for they shall find it.

Blessed are they who instead of trying to
batter down the gates of the kingdom of heaven
approach them humbly and lovingly and purified,
for they shall pass right through.

- Peace Pilgrim

Our Haven and Our Hope

Eternal Father bless our land,

179

Guard us with Thy Mighty Hand,

Keep us free from evil powers,

Be our light through countless hours.

To our Leaders, Great Defender,

Grant true wisdom from above. You are holy, Lord,
the only God,
and Your deeds are wonderful.

You are strong.

You are great.

You are the Most High.

You are Almighty.

You, Holy Father are King of heaven and earth.

You are Three and One, Lord God, all Good.

You are Good, all Good, supreme Good, Lord God, living and true.

You are love.

You are wisdom.

You are humility.

You are endurance.

You are rest.

You are peace.

You are joy and gladness.

You are justice and moderation.

You are all our riches, and You suffice for us.

You are beauty.

You are gentleness.

You are our protector.

You are our guardian and defender.

You are our courage.

You are our haven and our hope.

You are our faith, our great consolation.

You are our eternal life, Great and Wonderful Lord,

God Almighty, Merciful Savior.

- *St. Francis of Assisi*

True Wisdom from Above

Justice, Truth be ours forever,

Jamaica, land we love.

Jamaica, Jamaica, Jamaica, land we love.

Teach us true respect for all,

Stir response to duty's call,

strengthen us the weak to cherish,

Give us vision lest we perish.

Knowledge send us, Heavenly Father,

Grant true wisdom from above.

Justice, Truth be ours forever,

Jamaica, land we love.

Jamaica, Jamaica, Jamaica, land we love.

- Jamaican National Anthem

Discover What Is Truly Important in Life

In humility is the greatest freedom.

As long as you have to defend the imaginary self
that you think is important, you lose your peace of heart.

As soon as you compare that shadow
with the shadows of other people, you lose all joy,

because you have begun to trade in unrealities
and there is no joy in things that do not exist.

- Thomas Merton, 1961

September

Harvesting
Your Blessings

"Just think how happy you would be if you lost everything you have right now, and then got it back again."
—Frances Rodman

"Don't cry because it's over, smile because it happened."
—Dr. Seuss

"You must do the thing you think you cannot do."
—Eleanor Roosevelt

"I didn't fail the test, I just found 100 ways to do it wrong."
—Benjamin Franklin

Dancing With Angels

The angels dance in your wake

The sun rises for your glory

Stars illume in your light

Magnificent and eternal

My Lord Jesus

My timeless love

- Justin Pernette

A Love Perfected

AND GOD SAID TO THE SOUL:

I desired you before the world began.
I desire you now as you desire me.
And where the desires of two come together
The love is perfected.

HOW THE SOUL SPEAKS TO THE GOD:

Lord, you are my lover, my longing,
My flowing stream, my sun,
And I am your reflection.

HOW GOD ANSWERS THE SOUL:

185

It is my nature that makes me love you often,
For I am love itself.
It is my longing that makes me love you intensely,
For I yearn to be loved from the heart.
It is my eternity that makes me love you long,
For I have no end.

- Mechthild of Magdeburg, 13th Century

Sincerity of the Heart

To surrender oneself is something more
than to devote oneself, more than to give oneself,
it is even more than to abandon oneself to God.

To surrender oneself is to die to everything and to self,
to keep it continually turned towards God.

Self-surrender is no longer to seek self-satisfaction in anything
but solely God's good pleasure.

It should be added that self-surrender is to follow
that complete spirit of detachment
which holds to nothing;
neither to persons nor to things,
neither to time nor to place.

It means to accept everything, to submit to everything.

But perhaps you will think this is a difficult thing.

Do not let yourself be deceived; there is nothing so easy to do nothing so sweet to put into practice.

The whole thing consists in making a generous act at the very beginning,

by saying with all the sincerity of your heart:

"My God, I wish to be entirely thine; deign to accept my offering"

– then all is said. ...

You must always remember that you have surrendered yourself.

- St. Thérèse Couderc, 1864

There Is No Right Way to Pray—Just Do It

Sometimes it seems when I'm talking to people about prayer that one of the main points I have to keep making over and over is there is no right way. The important thing is to find your way...

...you don't need any kind of noble or highfalutin' or serious reason. Any reason to begin a pattern of prayer is a good reason because prayer is about everyday life.

- Roberta Bondi

Love Eternal

O Give thanks unto the Lord;
for he is good:
for his mercy endureth for ever.

- Psalm 118:1, KJV

Know Thyself, Know Myself

And a man said, speak to us of Self-Knowledge.

And he answered, saying:

Your hearts know in silence the secrets of the days and the nights.

But your ears thirst for the sound of your heart's knowledge.

You would know in words that
which you have always known in thought.

You would touch with your fingers the naked body of your dreams.

And it is well you should.

The hidden well-spring of your soul must needs
rise and run murmuring to the sea;

And the treasure of your infinite depths
would be revealed to your eyes.

But let there be no scales to weigh your unknown treasure;

And seek not the depths of your knowledge
with staff or sounding line.

For self is a sea boundless and measureless.

Say not, "I have found the truth",
but rather, "I have found a truth."

Say not, "I have found the path of the soul."

Say rather, "I have met the soul walking upon my path."

For the soul walks upon all paths.

The soul walks not upon a line, neither does it grow like a reed.

The soul unfolds itself, like a lotus of countless petals.

- Kahlil Gibran

Lifting Up the Lowly

My soul proclaims the greatness of the Lord;
My spirit rejoices in God my savior.

For he has looked upon his handmaid's lowliness;
behold, from now on will all ages call me blessed.

The Mighty One has done great things for me, and holy is
his name.

His mercy is from age to age to those who fear him.

He has shown might with his arm,
dispersed the arrogant of mind and heart.

He has thrown down the rulers from their thrones
but lifted up the lowly.

The hungry he has filled with good things;
the rich he has sent away empty.

He has helped Israel his servant, remembering his mercy,
According to his promise to our fathers,
to Abraham and to his descendants forever.

- Luke 1:46-55, CSB

Whosoever Shall Know Himself Shall Find It

Jesus saith,

Ye ask, who are those that draw us to the kingdom
if the kingdom is in Heaven?

... the fowls of the air and all beasts that are under
the earth or upon the earth and the fishes of the sea,
these are they which draw you
and the kingdom of Heaven is within you
and whosoever shall know himself shall find it.

Strive therefore to know yourselves and ye shall be aware
that ye are the sons of the Almighty Father; and ye shall know
that ye are in the city of God and ye are the city.

- Dead Sea Scrolls, Sayings of Jesus

Teach Your Children Well

O God! Educate these children.

These children are the plants of Thine orchard,
the flowers of Thy meadow,
the roses of Thy garden.

Let Thy rain fall upon them;
let the Sun of Reality shine upon them with Thy love.

Let Thy breeze refresh them in order
that they may be trained, grow, and develop,
and appear in the utmost beauty.

Thou art the Giver.

Thou art the Compassionate.

- `Abdu'l-bahá

Life Is Short, Don't Blow It

Life is like a blink of an eye,

Death is for eternity.

Therefore, life is really just a dream,

And death is the reality.

- Betty Pritchard, 1905

Peace, Love, and Understanding

God,

Please put a guard at my mouth,
love in my heart
and calm in my mind.

Amen.

- Julie Lepianka

Secret Teachings of Jesus

Jesus said,
Come, that I may teach you about
secrets no person has ever seen.

For there exists a great and boundless realm,
whose extent no generation of angels has seen,
in which there is a great invisible Spirit,
which no eye of an angel has ever seen,

no thought of the heart has ever comprehended,
and it was never called by any name.

- The Gospel of Judas

Saved by Love

Nothing that is worth doing can be achieved in our lifetime;
therefore, we must be saved by hope.

Nothing which is true or beautiful or good makes complete sense
in any immediate context of history;
therefore, we must be saved by faith.

Nothing we do, however virtuous, could be accomplished alone;
therefore, we must be saved by love.

No virtuous act is quite as virtuous from the standpoint of our
friend or foe as it is from our own standpoint;
therefore, we must be saved by the final form of love, which
is forgiveness.

- Reinhold Niebuhr, 1952

Give Me Your Love and I'll Be Rich Enough

Receive, O Lord, all my liberty.

Take my memory, my understanding, and my entire will.

Whatsoever I have or hold, You have given me;

I give it all back to You and surrender it
wholly to be governed by your will.

Give me only your love and your grace,
with these I will be rich enough,
and ask for nothing more.

- St. Ignatius Loyola, 16th Century

Within the Sanctuary of Thy Protection

I have awakened in Thy shelter, O my God,
and it becometh him that seeketh that shelter
to abide within the Sanctuary of Thy Protection
and the Stronghold of Thy defense.

Illumine my inner being, O my Lord,
with the splendors of the Dayspring of Thy Revelation,
even as Thou didst illumine my outer being
with the morning light of Thy favor.

- Baha'i Prayers

My Whole Life Becomes a Prayer

When I am liberated by silence,
when I am no longer involved
in the measurement of life, but in the living of it,

I can discover a form of prayer in which
there is effectively no distraction.

My whole life becomes a prayer.

My whole silence is full of prayer.

The world of silence in which I am immersed
contributes to my prayer.

- Thomas Merton

Prayer for Those Who May Lose Their Home

Father God, you are our provider. You promise protection and provision for us, so we come to you today asking for immediate and practical help for all those at risk of losing their homes. Some of these financial problems were not caused by any individual; some perhaps were the results of unwise decisions. Either way, at this point Lord, we need and ask for your intervention and help. We ask for practical relief and a specific solution to the problem. Bring the right people together to solve this housing crisis in a creative and timely way. Provide a way to pay this debt, or remove or realign or restructure the debt. Whatever will prove the best and right course, do it, Lord! Father, bring hope and faith and a relief from fear and a sense of despair. You promise in the Bible to "make a way where there is no way." This is time for that kind of miracle! Cut a new path through this impossible jungle. Save, and then bless this home! Your name is "Provider."

- Catholic Charities of Santa Rosa

When You Wake Up Empty and Frightened

Today, like every other day,
we wake up empty and frightened.

Don't open the door to the study and begin reading.

Take down a musical instrument.

Let the beauty we love be what we do.

There are a hundred ways to kneel and kiss the ground.

- Jelaluddin Rumi

May We All Have Peace

Praise ye, Ngai ... Peace be with us.

Say that the elders may have wisdom and speak with one voice.
Peace be with us.

Say that the country may have tranquility.
Peace be with us.

And the people may continue to increase.
Peace be with us.

Say that the people and the flock and the herds
May prosper and be free from illness.
Peace be with us.

Say that the fields may bear much fruit
And the land may continue to be fertile.
Peace be with us.

May peace reign over earth,
May the gourd cup agree with vessel.
Peace be with us.

May their heads agree and every ill word be driven out
Into the wilderness, into the virgin forest.

Praise ye, Ngai ... Peace be with us.

- Kenyan Song for Peace

Make America Grateful Again

Thou kind Lord!

This gathering is turning to Thee.

These hearts are radiant with Thy love.

These minds and spirits are exhilarated by
the message of Thy glad-tidings.

O God! Let this American democracy
become glorious in spiritual degrees even as
it has aspired to material degrees,
and render this just government victorious.

Confirm this revered nation to upraise
the standard of the oneness of humanity,
to promulgate the Most Great Peace,
to become thereby most glorious and praiseworthy
among all the nations of the world.

O God! This American nation is worthy of Thy favors
and is deserving of Thy mercy.

Make it precious and near to Thee
through Thy bounty and bestowal.

- `Abdu'l-bahá*

Make Haste To Be Kind

Life is short and we have not too much time
for gladdening the hearts of those
who are traveling the dark way with us.

Oh, be swift to love! Make haste to be kind.

- *Henri-Frederic Amiel, 1885*

Help Me To Not Be Negative

I am one with my father and the universe.

I am one with mother earth.

I am one with everyone within the reach of my voice.

And, in this togetherness, we ask the divine intelligence to
eradicate all
negatives from our hearts, from our minds,
from our words, and from our actions.

And so be it.

- Babatunde Olatunji

There Are Blessings Everywhere

Blessed is the spot,
and the house,
and the place,
and the city,
and the heart,
and the mountain,
and the refuge,
and the cave,
and the valley,
and the land,
and the sea,

and the island,
and the meadow
where mention of God hath been made
and His praise glorified.

- Anonymous

In Times of Great Trouble

I cried out to the Lord in my great trouble,
and he answered me.

I called to you from the land of the dead,
and Lord, you heard me!

I sank beneath the waves,
and the waters closed over me.

Seaweed wrapped itself around my head.

I sank down to the very roots of the mountains.

I was imprisoned in the earth,
whose gates lock shut forever.

But you, O Lord my God,
snatched me from the jaws of death!

As my life was slipping away,

I remembered the Lord.

And my earnest prayer went out to you
in your holy Temple.

- Jonah 2:2, 5-7

God Is With Us Always

In the beginning was God,

Today is God,

Tomorrow will be God.

Who can make an image of God?

He has no body.

He is the word which comes out of your mouth.

That word!

It is no more,

It is past, and still it lives!

So is God.

- African Tribal Pygmy Prayer

Walking Humbly with God

Rabbi Jesus the Messiah teaches me
to live fully
to act justly
to love tenderly
to walk humbly with my God and
where necessary to lose graciously.

- Alan Kaufman

May the Angels Care for the Sick and Dying

Watch thou, dear Lord,
with those who wake, or watch, or weep tonight,
and give thine angels charge over those who sleep.

Tend thy sick ones, Lord Christ.

Rest thy weary ones.

Bless thy dying ones.

Soothe thy suffering ones.

Pity thine afflicted ones.

Shield thy joyous ones.

And all, for thy love's sake.

Amen..

- Saint Augustine

All Religions, All This Singing, One Song

Move beyond any attachment to names. Every war
and every conflict between human beings has happened because
of some disagreement about
names. It's such an unnecessary foolishness, because just
beyond the arguing there's a long
table of companionship, set and waiting for us to sit down.

What is praised is one, so the praise is one too,
many jugs being poured
into a huge basin. All religions, all this singing,
one song.

The differences are just illusion and vanity. Sunlight
looks slightly different
on this wall than it does on that wall and a lot different
on this other one, but
it is still one light. We have borrowed these clothes, these
time-and-space personalities, from a light, and
when we praise, we pour them back in.

- Jelaluddin Rumi

O Thou,

the Sustainer of
our bodies, hearts, and souls,
Bless all
that we thankfully
receive.

Amen.

- Hazrat Inayat Khan

Your Heart is a Beating Drum

I am the drum,
you are the drum, and we are the drum.

Rhythm is the soul of life.
The whole universe revolves in rhythm.
Everything and every human action revolves in rhythm.

- Babatunde Olatunji

October

Gather Together with Friends and Family

"Count your age by friends, not years. Count your life by smiles, not tears."
—John Lennon

"You don't have to control your thoughts; you just have to stop letting them control you."
—Dan Millman

"Life isn't about waiting for the storm to pass, it's about learning how to dance in the rain."
—Vivian Greene

"Challenges are what make life interesting, and overcoming them is what makes life meaningful."
—Joshua J. Marine

My Guide and My Refuge

O God!
Refresh and gladden my spirit.
Purify my heart.
Illumine my powers.
I lay all my affairs in Thy hands.
Thou art my Guide and my Refuge.
I will no longer be sorrowful and grieved;
I will be a happy and joyful being.
O God! I will no longer be full of anxiety,
nor will I let trouble harass me.
I will not dwell on the unpleasant things of life.
O God! Thou art more friend to me than I am to myself.
I dedicate myself to Thee, O Lord.

- Kimberly Lynn Davis

Crying for Connection

The grief you cry out from
draws you toward union.

Your pure sadness
that wants help
is the secret cup.

Listen to the moan of a dog for its master.
That whining is the connection.

There are love dogs
no one knows the names of.

Give your life
to be one of them.

- Jelaluddin Rumi

Taking Comfort in Communion

O my God, O my Lord, O my Master!
I beg Thee to forgive me for seeking any pleasure save Thy love,
or any comfort except Thy nearness,
or any delight besides Thy good-pleasure,
or any existence other than communion with Thee.

- The Báb

Canticle of Brother Sun and Sister Moon

Most High, all-powerful, all-good Lord, all praise is Yours, all
glory, all honor and all blessings. To you alone, Most High, do they
belong, and no mortal lips are worthy to pronounce Your Name.

Praised be You, my Lord with all Your creatures, especially Sir
Brother Sun, who is the day through whom You give us light. And
he is beautiful and radiant with great splendor—of You Most High,
he bears the likeness.

Praised be You, my Lord, through Sister Moon and the stars, in the heavens you have made them bright, precious, and fair.

Praised be You, my Lord, through Brothers Wind and Air, and fair and stormy, all weather's moods, by which You cherish all that You have made.

Praised be You, my Lord, through Sister Water, so useful, humble, precious and pure.

Praised be You, my Lord, through Brother Fire, through whom You light the night, and he is beautiful and playful and robust and strong.

Praised be You, my Lord, through our Sister, Mother Earth, who sustains and governs us, producing varied fruits with colored flowers and herbs. Praise be to You, my Lord, through those who grant pardon for love of You and bear sickness and trial. Blessed are those who endure in peace, by You, Most High.

Praised be You, my Lord, through Sister Death, from whom no-one living can escape. Woe to those who die in mortal sin! Blessed are they She finds doing Your Will. No second death can do them harm. Praise and bless my Lord and give Him thanks, and serve Him with great humility.

- St. Francis of Assisi

The Gift of Humility

Do not seek too much fame,
but do not seek obscurity.
Be proud.
But do not remind the world of your deeds.
Excel when you must,
but do not excel the world.
Many heroes are not yet born,
many have already died.
To be alive to hear this song is a victory.

- Song from West Africa

One Love

I go into
the Muslim mosque
and the Jewish synagogue
and the Christian church
and I see one
altar.

- Allen Ginsberg

Prayer for Bedtime

Now I lay me down to sleep,
I pray the Lord my soul to keep.
If I should die before I wake,
I pray the Lord my soul to take.

- Author Unknown

Lift Your Voice in Thanks for His Love

Oludumare, oh Divine One! I give thanks
to You, the one who is as near as my
heartbeat, and more anticipated than my
next breath. Let Your wisdom become one
with this vessel as I lift my voice in
thanks for Your love.

- Yoruban Chant

Unite Our Hearts

O my God! O my God!
Unite the hearts of Thy servants,
and reveal to them Thy great purpose.
May they follow Thy commandments
and abide in Thy law.
Help them, O God, in their endeavor,

and grant them strength to serve Thee. O God!
Leave them not to themselves
but guide their steps by the light of Thy knowledge,
and cheer their hearts by Thy love.
Verily, Thou art their Helper and their Lord.

- Bahá'u'lláh

Practice Kindness Day and Night

May we practice kindness day and night,
forever, not only towards friends, but also to
strangers, and especially to the enemy;
not only towards human beings,
but also to animals and other beings
who want happiness and don't want to suffer.

May we constantly enjoy our lives by rejoicing.

May we constantly enjoy happiness
by rejoicing in all the positive things that bring
benefit to others and to ourselves.
And may we especially rejoice when we see
all the good things that happen to others.

May we develop patience to achieve all happiness,
temporal and ultimate, and to bring that
happiness to others; not only to our family,
but to all sentient beings.

May we develop all the 16 human qualities,
an understanding which makes our lives different.

May we become skilled in not harming sentient beings,
and may we become only the source of happiness
for sentient beings, like sunshine.

May we practice contentment.

May we learn contentment and satisfaction
an understanding which makes our lives different.

May we learn contentment and satisfaction.
May we learn to enjoy contentment,
which brings great freedom into our lives
and brings us so much happiness.
May we be an example to the world.

May we practice these good qualities
and when somebody abuses or harms us,
may we immediately forgive them.
In daily life, when we make mistakes and harm others,
may we immediately ask forgiveness.

May we be able to develop courage,
to be an inspiring example
and to be of benefit in so many ways for
the happiness of others, not only for ourselves.

- *Lama Zopa Rinpoche*

Prayer for Peaceful Sleep

Keep far from me at night
All things that me affright
And wake me safe with sunshine bright
within my heart;
If not within my sight.

- Doris Howe

By the Grace of God

God is Great, God is Good;
Let us thank Him for our food.
By His hands we all are fed,
Give us, Lord, our Daily Bread.
Amen..

- Author Unknown

God Bless Us, Every One

Little Boy kneels at the foot of the bed,
Droops on the little hands little gold head.
Hush! Hush! Whisper who dares!
Christopher Robin is saying his prayers.

God bless Mummy. I know that's right.
Wasn't it fun in the bath tonight?

The cold's so cold, and the hot's so hot.
Oh! God bless Daddy—I quite forgot.

If I open my fingers a little bit more,
I can see Nanny's dressing gown on the door.
It's a beautiful blue, but it hasn't a hood.
Oh! God bless Nanny and make her good.

Mine has a hood and if I lie in bed,
And put the hood right over my head,
And I shut my eyes, and I curl up small,
Nobody knows that I'm there at all.

Oh! Thank you, God, for a lovely day.
And what was the other I had to say?
I said "Bless Daddy," so what can it be?
Oh! Now I remember. God bless Me.

Little boy kneels at the foot of the bed,
Droops on the little hands little gold head,
Hush! Hush! Whisper who dares!
Christopher Robin is saying his prayers.

- Alan Alexander Milne

Thank You For Making This World

Goodnight God.
I hope you are having
a good time being the world.

I like the world very much
I'm glad you made the plants
and trees survive with the
rain and summers.
When summer is nearly near
the leaves begin to fall.
I hope you have a good time
being the world.
I like how God feels around
everyone in the world.
God, I am very happy that
I live on you.
Your arms clasp around the world.

- Louise Baxter

Prayer is Action

When you pray,
move your feet.

- African Proverb

Live With Courage

Silence becomes the son of a prince,
To be silent but brave in battle:

efits a man to be merry and glad
Until the day of his death.

coward believes he will live forever
If he holds back in the battle,
But in old age he shall have no peace
Though spears have spared his limbs.

- The Edda, 6th Century

Bloom Where You Are Planted

I am, O my God,
but a tiny seed which Thou hast sown
in the soil of Thy love,
and caused to spring forth by the hand of Thy bounty.
This seed craveth, therefore,
in its inmost being,
the waters of Thy mercy
and the living fountain of Thy grace.
Send down upon it,
from the heaven of Thy loving-kindness,
that which will enable it to flourish beneath Thy shadow
and within the borders of Thy court.
Thou art He Who watereth the hearts of all
that have recognized Thee from Thy plenteous stream
and the fountain of Thy living waters.

Praised be to God,
the Lord of the worlds.

- Medieval Chant

Living Life as a Thank You

Thank you for the world so sweet,
Thank you for the food we eat.
Thank you for the birds that sing,
Thank you, God, for everything.

- Grace for Mealtime

Blessing for the Daily Meal

Thank you, God, for food so good,
and help us do the things we should.

Help us with our work and play,
and everything we do and say.
Amen..

- Author Unknown

Your Infinite Peace

Center of all centers, core of cores,
almond self-enclosed and growing sweet-
all this universe, to the furthest stars
and beyond them, is your flesh, your fruit.

Now you feel how nothing clings to you;
your vast shell reaches into endless space,
and there the rich, thick fluids rise and flow,
Illuminated in your infinite peace.

A billion stars go spinning through the night,
blazing high above your head.
But in you is the presence that
will be, when all the stars are dead.

- Rainer Maria Rilke

Sweet Sleep, Sweet Dreams for All

Bless me, Lord, this night I pray,

Keep me safe till dawn of day,
Bless my mother and my father,
Bless my sister and my brother,
Bless each little girl and boy,
Bless them all for heavenly joy.

Amen..

- Author Unknown

I Cannot Do This Alone

O God, early in the morning I cry to you.
Help me to pray
And to concentrate my thoughts on you:
I cannot do this alone.
In me there is darkness,
But with you there is light;
I am lonely, but you do not leave me;
I am feeble in heart, but with you there is help;
I am restless, but with you there is peace.
In me there is bitterness, but with you there is patience;
I do not understand your ways,
But you know the way for me...
Restore me to liberty,
And enable me to live now
That I may answer before you and before me.
Lord, whatever this day may bring,
Your name be praised.

- Dietrich Bonhoeffer

Medieval Nordic Blessing Song

Hail to thee, day! Hail, ye day's sons!
Hail, night and daughter of night!
With blithe eyes look on both of us:
send to those sitting here speed!

Hail to you, God! Hail!
Hail, earth that givest to all!
Goodly days and speech bespeak we from you,
and healing hands, in this life.

- The Poetic Edda—the Lay of Sigrdrifa, 600 AD

May My Heart Be Pure

Create in me a pure heart, O my God,
and renew a tranquil conscience within me, O my Hope!
Through the spirit of power confirm Thou me in Thy Cause,
O my Best-Beloved,
and by the light of Thy glory reveal unto me Thy path,
O Thou the Goal of my desire!
Through the power of Thy transcendent might
lift me up unto the heaven of Thy holiness,
O Source of my being,
and by the breezes of Thine eternity gladden me,
O Thou Who art my God!
Let Thine everlasting melodies breathe tranquility on me,
O my Companion,
and let the riches of Thine ancient countenance

deliver me from all except Thee,
O my Master,
and let the tidings of the revelation of Thine
incorruptible Essence bring me joy,
O Thou Who art the most manifest of the manifest
and the most hidden of the hidden!

- Walter Harmon

A Heart So Pure

O love, O pure deep love, be here, be now—be all;
Worlds dissolve into your stainless endless radiance,
Frail living leaves burn with you brighter than cold stars.
Make me your servant, your breath, your core.

- Sufi Song

Abraham Lincoln's Gettysburg Address

Four score and seven years ago
our fathers brought forth on this continent,
a new nation, conceived in Liberty,
and dedicated to the proposition that
all men are created equal.

Now we are engaged in a great civil war,
testing whether that nation, or any nation
so conceived and so dedicated, can long endure.

221

We are met on a great battle-field of that war.
We have come to dedicate a portion of that field,
as a final resting place for those who here
gave their lives that that nation might live.
It is altogether fitting and proper
that we should do this

But, in a larger sense, we cannot dedicate –
we cannot consecrate—we cannot hallow—this ground.
The brave men, living and dead, who struggled here,
have consecrated it far above our poor power to add or detract.
The world will little note nor long remember what we say here,
but it can never forget what they did here.
It is for us the living, rather, to be dedicated here
to the unfinished work which they
who fought here have thus far so nobly advanced.
It is rather for us to be here dedicated
to the great task remaining before us –
that from these honored dead we take increased devotion
to that cause for which they gave
the last full measure of devotion –
that we here highly resolve that
these dead shall not have died in vain –
that this nation, under God, shall have
a new birth of freedom –
and that government of the people,
by the people, for the people,
shall not perish from the earth.

- *To Heal the Nation After Civil War, November 19, 1863*

Being Thankful for Each New Challenge

Be thankful that you don't already have everything you desire,
If you did, what would there be to look forward to?

Be thankful when you don't know something
For it gives you the opportunity to learn.

Be thankful for the difficult times.
During those times you grow.

Be thankful for your limitations
Because they give you opportunities for improvement.

Be thankful for each new challenge
Because it will build your strength and character.

Be thankful for your mistakes
They will teach you valuable lessons.

Be thankful when you're tired and weary
Because it means you've made a difference.

It is easy to be thankful for the good things.
A life of rich fulfillment comes to those who are
also thankful for the setbacks.

Gratitude can turn a negative into a positive.

Find a way to be thankful for your troubles
and they can become your blessing.

- Anonymous

A Spirit to Know You

Gracious and Holy Father,
Please give me:
intellect to understand you,
reason to discern you,
diligence to seek you,
wisdom to find you,
a spirit to know you,
a heart to meditate upon you,
ears to hear you,
eyes to see you,
a tongue to proclaim you,
a way of life pleasing to you,
patience to wait for you
and perseverance to look for you.

Grant me a perfect end,
your holy presence,
a blessed resurrection
and life everlasting.

Amen..

- St. Benedict of Nursiaca, 480-547

May Your Heart's Wishes Soon Be Fulfilled

Just as the soft rains fill the streams,
pour into the rivers and join together in the oceans,

---

so may the power of every moment of your goodness
flow forth to awaken and heal all beings,
Those here now, those gone before, those yet to come.

By the power of every moment of your goodness
May your heart's wishes be soon fulfilled
as completely shining as the bright full moon,
as magically as by a wish-fulfilling gem.

By the power of every moment of your goodness
May all dangers be averted and all disease be gone.
May no obstacle come across your way.
May you enjoy fulfillment and long life.

For all in whose heart dwells respect,
who follow the wisdom and compassion of the Way,
May your life prosper in the four blessings
of old age, beauty, happiness and strength.

- Traditional Buddhist Blessing and Healing Chant

The Power of Kindness

Kindness in words creates confidence,
Kindness in thinking creates profoundness,
Kindness in giving creates love.

- Lao Tzu

Thank You, Lord, for Renewing My Strength

You are my rock, and I run to you today believing that you will lift up my heavy arms, that you will fuel me for the tasks you've given me, and that your joy will completely consume the weakness of my life and make me strong again. I don't want to stay grounded, crippled by limitations and failed attempts. I'm tired of feeble efforts. Lord, I want to mount up with wings like an eagle and not just fly. I want to soar.

Renew my strength, Lord. Fill me with your supernatural power to overcome each obstacle in my path. With my eyes on you, Lord, with you walking beside me, working through me, I can make it. Thank you, Lord!

In Jesus' name, Amen..

- Helen Baxter Harmon

November

Count Your Blessings and Be Thankful

"Gratitude and esteem are good foundations of affection."
—Jane Austen

"'Enough is a feast."
—Buddhist Proverb

"When you arise in the morning, think of what a precious privilege it is to be alive—to breathe, to think, to enjoy, to love."
—Marcus Aurelius

"I have found that worry and irritation vanish the moment when I open my mind to the many blessings that I possess."
—Dale Carnegie

Love for Every Living Creature

May every creature abound in well-being and peace.
May every living being, weak or strong, the long and the small,
The short and the medium-sized, the mean and the great;
May every living being, seen or unseen, those dwelling far off,
Those nearby, those already born, those waiting to be born;
May all attain inward peace.

Let no one deceive another.
Let no one despise another in any situation.
Let no one, from antipathy or hatred, wish evil to anyone at all.
Just as a mother, with her own life,
protects her only son from hurt,
So within yourself foster a limitless concern
for every living creature.

Display a heart of boundless love for all the world.
In all its height and depth and broad extent,
Love unrestrained, without hate or enmity.
Then as you stand or walk, sit or lie,
until overcome by drowsiness
Devote your mind entirely to this,
it is known as living here life divine.

- Traditional Blessing by the Buddha

All Things Calm

You are the peace of all things calm
You are the place to hide from harm
You are the light that shines in the dark
You are the heart's eternal spark
You are the door that's open wide
You are the guest who waits inside
You are the stranger at the door
You are the calling of the poor
You are my Lord and save me from ill
You are the light, the truth, the way
You are my Savior this very day.

- Medieval Celtic Chant

Thine Aid We Seek

Praise be to Allah, the Cherisher and Sustainer of the worlds
Most Gracious, Most Merciful; Master of the Day of Judgment.
Thee do we worship, and Thine aid we seek.
Show us the straight way,
The way of those on whom Thou hast bestowed Thy Grace,
those whose (portion) is not wrath, and who go not astray.

- Sufi Lord's Prayer

For Help During A Natural Disaster

Dear God,

Right now, Lord, we are not at peace. We are in the middle of
a fallen world, where there are natural disasters and crushed
dreams, where we're surrounded by heartbreaks and sorrow and
death. We watch them on the news, we see them in the lives of our
friends and family, we feel them in our own hearts.

To be honest, it's easier sometimes just to give up. To choose
bitterness or fear or anger and run away from others and from you.
But you call us to draw near in times of suffering. Give us courage
to pray for that in our lives and those around us when we're
tempted to give up or turn away from you. When our prayers are
answered with "no," or even a time of silence, draw us in. Remind
us of your love. Bring others around us to speak truth even when
we can't yet feel it.

- *CrossTalk*

Give Me Strength for Today and Hope
for Tomorrow

God, hear my prayer,
And let my cry come to You.
Do not hide from me in the day of my distress;
Turn to me and speedily answer my prayer.
Eternal God, Source of healing,
Out of my distress I call upon You.

Help me sense Your presence
At this difficult time.
Grant me patience when the hours are heavy;
In hurt or disappointment give me courage.
Keep me trustful in Your love.
Give me strength for today, and hope for tomorrow.
To your loving hands I commit my spirit
When asleep and when awake. You are with me; I shall not fear

- Traditional Jewish Healing Prayer

Read Your Own Heart Right

We would have inward peace,
Yet will not look within;
We would have misery cease,
Yet will not cease from sin;

Once, read your own heart right
And you will have done with fears;
Man gets no other light
Though he search a thousand years.

- Matthew Arnold, 1852

Be an Expression of God's Love

Let my heart be the vessel of God's Love.

Let my thoughts be the blossom of God's Love.

Let my words be the expression of God's Love.

Let my actions be the fulfillment of God's Love.

- David Ridge

Finding Hope in the Darkness

Touch the pain of the world
and release hope into the darkness.

- Sisters of Social Service

Where Your Treasure Is, There Will Your Heart Be Also

Lay not up for yourselves
treasures upon the earth,
where moth and rust doth corrupt,
and where thieves break though and steal:

But lay up for yourselves
treasures in heaven,
where neither moth nor rust doth corrupt,
and where thieves do not break through nor steal:

For where your treasure is,
there will your heart be also.

- St. Matthew - 6:19–21, KJV

Shelter in Any Storm of Fear and Trouble

Almighty God, the Refuge of all that are distressed, grant unto
us that in all trouble of this our mortal life, we may flee to the
knowledge of Thy lovingkindness and tender mercy; that so,
sheltering ourselves therein, the storms of life may pass over us,
and not shake the peace of God that is within us. Whatsoever this
life may bring us, grant that it may never take from us the full faith
that Thou art our Father. Grant us Thy light, that we may have life,
through Jesus Christ our Lord. Amen..

- George Dawson

Transforming Pain to Joy

May God bless you with a restless discomfort
about easy answers, half-truths and superficial relationships,
so that you may seek truth boldly and love deep within your heart.

May God bless you with holy anger at injustice, oppression,
and exploitation of people, so that you may tirelessly work for
justice, freedom, and peace among all people.

May God bless you with the gift of tears to shed with those who
suffer
from pain, rejection, starvation, or the loss of all that they cherish,
so that you may
reach out your hand to comfort them and transform their pain
into joy.

May God bless you with enough foolishness to believe that
you really CAN make a difference in this world, so that you are
able,
with God's grace, to do what others claim cannot be done.

And the blessing of God the Supreme Majesty and our Creator,
Jesus Christ the Incarnate Word who is our brother and Savior,
and the Holy Spirit, our Advocate and Guide, be with you
and remain with you, this day and forevermore.

Amen..

- *Benedictine Blessing*

Lift Me Up

My Lord, I know not what I ought to ask of Thee.
Thou and Thou alone knowest my needs.
Thou lovest me more than I am able to love Thee.
O Father, grant unto me, Thy servant, all which I cannot ask.
For a cross I dare not ask, nor for consolation;
I dare only to stand in Thy presence.
My heart is open to Thee.

Thou seest my needs of which I myself am unaware.
Behold and lift me up!
In Thy presence I stand,
awed and silenced by Thy will and Thy judgments,
into which my mind cannot penetrate.
To Thee I offer myself as a sacrifice.
No other desire is mine but to fulfill Thy will.
Teach me how to pray.
Do Thyself pray within me.
Amen..

- Prayer of Philaret, Moscow: 1782–1867

Coming Together—Growing Together

We light the light of a new idea.
It is the light of our coming together.
It is the light of our growing;
to know new things,
to see new beauty,
to feel new love.

- Unitarian Chalice Lighting Invocation

235

Prayer for Help When Caring for Aged and Infirm Parents

Lord, when we are infants, you partner with our parents in loving and caring for us. My parent(s) is (are) now elderly and infirm, and I ask that you partner with me in giving (her, him, them) the same tender loving care. Give me the strength to be fully present for my (mother, father, parents) and lovingly tend to (her, his, their) needs and the wisdom to take time out to tend to my physical, emotional, and spiritual needs as I care for (her, him, them).
Amen..

- Holy Names Chapel

Comfort in Sickness

Heavenly Father
I call on you. I ask you to touch [us] with your healing power.
Cast out all sickness and recreate [us].
Let the warmth of your healing love pass through [us].
Lord grant that [we] will be free from pain,
from anxiety, and from discomfort.
Please allow your love and the compassion of caregivers,
family and friends to bring peace and comfort to [us].
This we ask through Christ, our Lord.
Amen.

- Walter Whitmore

Prayer for Farm Workers' Struggle

Show me the suffering of the most miserable;
So I will know my people's plight.

Free me to pray for others;
For you are present in every person.

Help me take responsibility for my own life;
So that I can be free at last.

Grant me courage to serve others;
For in service there is true life.

Give me honesty and patience;
So that the Spirit will be alive among us.

Let the Spirit flourish and grow;
So that we will never tire of the struggle.

Let us remember those who have died for justice;
For they have given us life.

Help us love even those who hate us;
So we can change the world.
Amen..

- César Chávez

Deliver Me

Dear God,
Deliver me to my passion.
Deliver me to my brilliance.
Deliver me to my intelligence.
Deliver me to my depth.
Deliver me to my nobility.
Deliver me to my beauty.
Deliver me to my power to heal.
Deliver me to You.

- Marianne Williamson

In A World Without End

For this cause I bow my knees
unto the Father of our Lord Jesus Christ,

Of Whom the whole family in heaven and earth is named,

That He would grant you, according to the riches of His glory,
to be strengthened with might by His Spirit in the inner man;

That Christ may dwell in your hearts by faith;
that ye, being rooted and grounded in love,

May be able to comprehend with all saints
what is the breadth, and length, and depth, and height;

And to know the love of Christ, which passeth knowledge,
that ye might be filled with all the fullness of God.

Now unto Him that is able to do exceeding abundantly
above all that we ask or think,
according to the power that worketh in us,

Unto him be glory in the church by Christ Jesus
throughout all ages, world without end. Amen..

- Ephesians 3:14-21, Apostle Paul, KJV

Never Give Up

We are pressed on every side by troubles, but we are not crushed
and broken. We are perplexed, but we don't give up and quit.
That is why we never give up. Though our bodies are dying, our
spirits are being renewed every day. For our present troubles are
quite small and won't last very long. Yet they produce for us an
immeasurably great glory that will last forever!

- 2 Corinthians 4:8, 16-17, TLB

Novena to Saint Jude

Sacred heart of Jesus be adored
glorified, loved and preserved
throughout the world
now and forever.

Sacred heart of Jesus pray for us.
St. Jude, worker of miracles, pray for us.
St. Jude, helper of the hopeless, pray for us.
thank you St. Jude.
Amen..

- Catholic Liturgy

For Honor and Duty in Service

Almighty, Everlasting God,
the Protector of all those who put their trust in Thee:
hear our prayers in behalf of Thy servants
who sail their vessels beneath the seas.
We beseech Thee to keep in Thy sustaining care
all who are in submarines,
that they may be delivered
from the hidden dangers of the deep.
Grant them courage
and a devotion to fulfill their duties,
that they may better serve Thee and their native land.
Though acquainted with the depths of the ocean,
deliver them from the depths of despair
and the dark hours of the absence of friendliness
and grant them a good ship's spirit.
Bless all their kindred and loved ones
from whom they are separated.
When they surface their ships,
may they praise Thee, for Thou art there

as well as in the deep.
Fill them with Thy Spirit
that they may be sure in their reckonings,
unwavering in duty,
high in purpose,
and uphold the honor of their nation.

Amen.

- Submariner's Prayer, Anonymous

In Dangerous Weather

God, ransack the little ordered
rooms of my dignity, and cast
me out into wide and dangerous
weathers of my deepest needs.

- Author Unknown

Strength for the Journey

My True Father,
I set my hopes upon You alone,
And I only ask You, God,
For my Soul salvation.

Let Your Holy Will
Be my strengthening on this way,

For my life without You is a mere empty moment,
And only serving You leads to Eternal life.
Amen.!

- St. Agapit of Pechersk, 11th Century

A Prayer for Those Dealing with Alzheimer's Disease

Dear Lord,
For the many persons who have died
of Alzheimer's Disease, we pray that
they are in the care of your loving arms...
For those who are now victims of Alzheimer's
Disease, we pray for dignity and comfort...
For the Alzheimer's Disease caregivers,
we pray for compassion and patience...
For the Alzheimer's Disease families,
we pray for strength and courage...
For those who seek the cause, cure,
prevention, and treatment of Alzheimer's
Disease, we pray for your wisdom,

guidance, and direction, and
For the hope You have given us...
our thanks.

Amen.

- Grace Hospice

Mercy for Someone Suffering from Alzheimer's

Dear Lord,
Please grant my visitors tolerance for my confusion,
Forgiveness for my irrationality, and the strength
To walk with me into the mist of memory
My world has become.

Please let them take my hand and stay awhile,
Even though I seem unaware of their presence.
Help them to know how their strength
And loving care will drift slowly
Into the days to come just when I need it most.

Let them know when I don't recognize them
That I will. . . I will.
Keep their hearts free from sorrow for me,
For my sorrow, when it comes,
Only lasts a moment, when it's gone.

And finally Lord, please let them know,
How very much their visits mean,
How even through this relentless mystery,
I can still feel their love.

Amen.!

- Grace Hospice

For Those Who Need Employment

Heavenly Father, we remember before you those who suffer want and anxiety from lack of work. Guide the people of this land to use our public and private wealth so that all may find suitable and fulfilling employment and receive just payment for their labor; through Jesus Christ our Lord. Amen..

- Morning Star Church

Only Plowshares, No Swords

Imagine a small state with a small population
Let there be labor-saving tools
that aren't used
Let people consider death
and not move far
Let there be boats and carts
but no reason to ride them
Let there be armor and weapons
but no reason to employ them
Let people return to the use of knots
and be satisfied with their food
and pleased with their clothing
and content with their homes
and happy with their customs
Let there be another state so near
people hear its dogs and chickens

but live out their lives
without making a visit.

- Lao Tzu

Make Me a Miracle Worker

I am here only to be truly helpful.
I am here to represent Him Who sent me.
I do not have to worry about what to say or what to do,
because He Who sent me will direct me.
I am content to be wherever He wishes, knowing He goes there
with me.
I will be healed as I let Him teach me to heal.

- A Course in Miracles

The Golden Eternity

It said that Nothing Ever Happened, so don't worry.
It's all like a dream.
Everything is ecstasy, inside.
We just don't know it because of our thinking-minds.
But in our true blissful essence of mind is known
that everything is alright forever and forever and forever.
Close your eyes,
let your hands and nerve-ends drop,
stop breathing for 3 seconds,

listen to the silence inside the illusion of the world,
and you will remember the lesson you forgot which was taught in
immense milky ways
of cloudy innumerable worlds
long ago and not even at all.
It is all one vast awakened thing.
I call it the golden eternity.
It is perfect.

- Jack Kerouac

Mi Sheberakh; May the One Who Blessed

May the One who blessed our ancestors –
Patriarchs Abraham, Isaac, and Jacob,
Matriarchs Sarah, Rebecca, Rachel, and Leah –
bless and heal the one who is ill:
(name) son/daughter of (name) .

May the Holy Blessed One
overflow with compassion upon him/her,
to restore him/her,
to heal him/her,
to strengthen him/her,
to enliven him/her.

The One will send him/her, speedily,
a complete healing –
healing of the soul and healing of the body –
along with all the ill,

among the people of Israel and all humankind,

soon,

speedily,

without delay,

and let us all say:

Amen.

- Traditional Jewish Prayer for the Sick

December

Life is a Gift and Love is the Key

"When all seems lost, stop where you are and think of three things you are grateful for. You will feel much better immediately. Make this a morning prayer."
—Becca Anderson

"Gratitude is the state of mind of thankfulness. As it is cultivated, we experience an increase in our "sympathetic joy," our happiness at another's happiness. Just as in the cultivation of compassion, we may feel the pain of others, so we may begin to feel their joy as well. And it doesn't stop there."
—Stephen Levine

"Wake at dawn with a winged heart and give thanks for another day of loving."
—Kahlil Gibran

How Can We Be Our Best Selves

Great God, who has told us
"Vengeance is mine,"
save us from ourselves,
save us from the vengeance in our hearts
and the acid in our souls.

Save us from our desire to hurt as we have been hurt,
to punish as we have been punished,
to terrorize as we have been terrorized.

Give us the strength it takes
to listen rather than to judge,
to trust rather than to fear,
to try again and again
to make peace even when peace eludes us.

We ask, O God, for the grace
to be our best selves.
We ask for the vision
to be builders of the human community
rather than its destroyers.
We ask for the humility as a people
to understand the fears and hopes of other peoples.

We ask for the love it takes
to bequeath to the children of the world to come
more than the failures of our own making.
We ask for the heart it takes.

- Sister Joan Chittister

Give Your Hearts in Love

You were born together, and together you shall be forevermore.
You shall be together when white wings of death scatter your days.
Aye, you shall be together even in the silent memory of God.
But let there be spaces in your togetherness,
And let the winds of the heavens dance between you.
Love one another but make not a bond of love:
Let it rather be a moving sea between the shores of your souls.
Fill each other's cup, but drink not from one cup.
Give one another of your bread, but eat not from the same loaf.
Sing and dance together and be joyous, but let each one of you be
alone,
Even as the strings of a lute are alone though they quiver with the
same music.
Give your hearts, but not into each other's keeping.
For only the hand of Life can contain your hearts.
And stand together, yet not too near together:
For the pillars of the temple stand apart,
And the oak tree and the cypress grow not in each other's shadow.

- Kahlil Gibran

In This Miracle, All Miracles Are Born

A God becomes Child to save the children,
Shepherds chant with the tongue of Angels,
Salvation is described in a Mystery,
Heaven and Earth mingle into one Soul this night.

Prophecy is the point of a Star.
Cherubim bow with the neck of Shepherds.
A cave becomes the Gate of the Universe
While kings search for the bed of a Beggar.

A Maiden becomes the Mother of Grace;
Life has been given another Life.
The Child reaches out, takes hold of the world
And smiles the Innocent Smile.

In this Miracle all miracles are born –
The blind receive sight and the deaf have song,
The cold and homeless have shelter
And pilgrims cease their wanderings.

In this Creation all creation is born
And all creatures have a voice.
We find ourselves kneeling alongside the Magi.
The Child turns, looks and recognizes.

- Luke 2:11

Keep On the Sunny Side of Life

There's a dark and a troubled side of life;
There's a bright and a sunny side, too;
Tho' we meet with the darkness and strife,
The sunny side we also may view.

Keep on the sunny side, always on the sunny side,
Keep on the sunny side of life;
It will help us every day, it will brighten all the way,
If we keep on the sunny side of life.

Tho' the storm in its fury break today,
Crushing hopes that we cherished so dear,
Storm and cloud will in time pass away,
The sun again will shine bright and clear.

Keep on the sunny side, always on the sunny side,
Keep on the sunny side of life;
It will help us every day, it will brighten all the way,
If we keep on the sunny side of life.

Let us greet with a song of hope each day,
Tho' the moments be cloudy or fair;
Let us trust in our Savior always,
Who keepeth everyone in His care.

Keep on the sunny side, always on the sunny side,
Keep on the sunny side of life;
It will help us every day, it will brighten all the way,
If we keep on the sunny side of life.

- Carter Family song by Ada Blenkhorn, 1899

Teach Me To Serve As I Should

Dearest Lord, teach me to be generous,
teach me to serve you as I should,
to give and not to count the cost,
to fight and not to heed the wounds,
to toil and not to seek for rest,
to labor and ask not for reward,
save that of knowing that I do your most holy will.

- St. Ignatius Loyola, 1642

Allow God's Grace to Enter and Do the Rest

It helps, now and then, to step back and take a long view.
The kingdom is not only beyond our efforts, it is even beyond our
vision.
We accomplish in our lifetime only a tiny fraction
of the magnificent enterprise that is God's work.

Nothing we do is complete, which is a way of
saying that the Kingdom always lies beyond us.
No statement says all that could be said.
No prayer fully expresses our faith.
No confession brings perfection.
No pastoral visit brings wholeness.
No program accomplishes the Church's mission.
No set of goals and objectives includes everything.

This is what we are about. We plant the seeds that one day will
grow.
We water seeds already planted, knowing that they hold future
promise.
We lay foundations that will need further development.
We provide yeast that produces far beyond our capabilities.

We cannot do everything, and there is a sense of liberation in
realizing that.
This enables us to do something, and to do it very well.
It may be incomplete, but it is a beginning, a step along the way,
an opportunity for the Lord's grace to enter and do the rest.

We may never see the end results, but that is the difference
between the master builder and the worker.
We are workers, not master builders; ministers, not messiahs.
We are prophets of a future not our own.

- Bishop Ken Untener

Welcome Morning

There is joy
in all:
in the hair I brush each morning,
in the Cannon towel, newly washed,
that I rub my body with each morning,
in the chapel of eggs I cook
each morning,
in the outcry from the kettle

that heats my coffee
each morning,
in the spoon and the chair
that cry, "hello there, Anne,"
each morning,
in the godhead of the table
that I set my silver, plate, cup upon
each morning.

All this is God,
right here in my pea-green house
each morning
and I mean,
though often forget,
to give thanks,
to faint down by the kitchen table
in a prayer of rejoicing
as the holy birds at the kitchen window
peck into their marriage of seeds.

So while I think of it,
let me paint a thank-you on my palm
for this God, this laughter of the morning,
lest it go unspoken.

The Joy that isn't shared, I've heard,
dies young.

- Anne Sexton

I've Been to the Mountaintop

Well, I don't know what will happen now.
We've got some difficult days ahead.
But it doesn't matter with me now.
Because I've been to the mountaintop.
And I don't mind.
Like anybody, I would like to live a long life.
Longevity has its place.
But I'm not concerned about that now.
I just want to do God's will.
And He's allowed me to go up to the mountain.
And I've looked over.
And I've seen the promised land.
I may not get there with you.
But I want you to know tonight, that we,
as a people will get to the promised land.
And I'm happy, tonight.
I'm not worried about anything.
I'm not fearing any man.
Mine eyes have seen the glory of the coming of the Lord.

- Dr. Martin Luther King, Jr.

When You Are Feeling Burdened

I cast
every burden

on the Christ within
and I go free!

- Florence Scovel Shinn, 1925

Put Aside Your Care and Worry

All shall
be well,
and all shall
be well,
and all manner
of thing
shall be well.

- Julian of Norwich, 14th Century

You Are Guided, Guarded, and Protected

The light of God surrounds me;
The love of God enfolds me;
The power of God protects me;
The presence of God watches over me.
Wherever I am, God is.

- James Dillet Freeman, 1941

Be a Student of Life

May your journey
through the universal questions of life
bring you to a new moment of awareness.
May it be an enlightening one.

May you find embedded in the past,
like all the students of life before you,
the answers you are seeking now.

May they awaken that in you which is
deeper than fact,
truer than fiction,
full of faith.

May you come to know
that in every human event
is a particle of the Divine
to which we turn for meaning here,
to which we tend for fullness of life hereafter.

- Sr. Joan Chittister

Prayer for Healing

And God shall wipe away all tears from their eyes;
and there shall be no more death,
neither sorrow, nor crying,

neither shall there be any more pain;
for the former things are passed away.

- Revelation 21:4

Thank You God For This Most Amazing Morning

i thank You God for most this amazing
day: for the leaping greenly spirits of trees
and a blue true dream of sky; and for everything
which is natural which is infinite which is yes

(i who have died am alive again today,
and this is the sun's birthday; this is the birth
day of life and of love and wings: and of the gay
great happening illimitably earth)

how should tasting touching hearing seeing
breathing any—lifted from the no
of all nothing—human merely being
doubt unimaginable You?

(now the ears of my ears awake and
now the eyes of my eyes are opened)

- e. e. cummings

Faith, Hope and Love

Love is long-suffering,
love is kind,
it is not jealous,
love does not boast,
it is not inflated.

It is not discourteous,
it is not selfish,
it is not irritable,
it does not enumerate the evil.

It does not rejoice over the wrong,
but rejoices in the truth

It covers all things, it has faith for all things,
it hopes in all things, it endures in all things.

Love never falls in ruins;
but whether prophecies, they will be abolished; or
tongues, they will cease; or
knowledge, it will be superseded.

For we know in part and we prophecy in part.

But when the perfect comes, the imperfect will be superseded.

When I was an infant,
I spoke as an infant, I reckoned I spoke as an infant, I reckoned as
an infant;

when I became [an adult],
I abolished the things of the infant.

For now we see through a mirror in an enigma, but then face to
face.
Now I know in part, but then I shall know
as also I was fully known.

But now remains faith, hope, love, these three;
but the greatest of these is love.

- 1 Corinthians 13:1-13, NIV

Love Thee More Dearly, And Follow Thee More Nearly

Thanks be to thee, my Lord Jesus Christ,
For all the benefits thou hast won for me,
For all the pains and insults thou hast borne for me.

O most merciful Redeemer, Friend, and Brother,
May I know thee more clearly,
Love thee more dearly,
And follow thee more nearly:
For ever and ever.

- St. Richard of Chichester, 1197-1253

Pray About Everything

Always be full of joy in the Lord.
I say it again—rejoice!

Let everyone see that you are considerate in all you do.
Remember the Lord is coming soon.

Don't worry about anything,
instead pray about everything.
Tell God what you need,
and thank him for all he has done.

If you do this, you will experience God's peace,
which is far more wonderful
than the human mind can understand.
His peace will guard your hearts and minds
as you live in Christ Jesus.

- Philippians 4:4-7, NLT

Empty Your Heart of Fears

Do you need Me?
I am there.

You cannot see Me, yet I am the light you see by.
You cannot hear Me, yet I speak through your voice.
You cannot feel Me, yet I am the power at work in your hands.

I am at work, though you do not understand My ways.
I am at work, though you do not understand My works.

I am not strange visions. I am not mysteries.

Only in absolute stillness, beyond self, can you know Me
as I am, and then but as a feeling and a faith.

Yet I am there. Yet I hear. Yet I answer.
When you need Me, I am there.
Even if you deny Me, I am there.
Even when you feel most alone, I am there.
Even in your fears, I am there.
Even in your pain, I am there.

I am there when you pray and when you do not pray.
I am in you, and you are in Me.
Only in your mind can you feel separate from Me, for
only in your mind are the mists of "yours" and "mine."
Yet only with your mind can you know Me and experience Me.

Empty your heart of empty fears.
When you get yourself out of the way, I am there

You can of yourself do nothing, but I can do all.
And I am in all.

Though you may not see the good, good is there, for
I am there. I am there because I have to be, because I am.

Only in Me does the world have meaning;
only out of Me does the world take form;

only because of Me does the world go forward.
I am the law on which the movement of the stars
   and the growth of living cells are founded.

I am the love that is the law's fulfilling.
I am assurance.
I am peace.
I am oneness.
I am the law that you can live by.
I am the love that you can cling to.
I am your assurance.
I am your peace.
I am ONE with you.
I am.

Though you fail to find Me, I do not fail you.
Though your faith in Me is unsure,
My faith in you never wavers,
because I know you, because I love you.

Beloved, I AM there.

- James Dillet Freeman, 1947

Help Us to Do the Things We Should

Father, we thank thee for the night,
and for the pleasant morning light;
for rest and food and loving care,
and all that makes the day so fair.

Help us to do the things we should,
to be to others kind and good;
in all we do, in work or play,
to grow more loving every day.

- Rebecca Weston, 1890

Live the Questions Now

Have patience with everything unresolved in your heart
and try to love the questions themselves ...
Don't search for the answers,
which could not be given to you now,
because you would not be able to live them.
And the point is to live everything.
Live the questions now.
Perhaps then, someday far in the future,
you will gradually, without even noticing it,
live your way into the answer.

- Rainer Maria Rilke

Give Thanks for Everything

For each new morning with its light,
For rest and shelter of the night,
For health and food,

For love and friends,
For everything Thy goodness sends.

- Ralph Waldo Emerson

Bring the Gift of Gladness to Others

Almighty God, thank Thee for the job of this day.
May we find gladness in all its toil and difficulty,
its pleasure and success,
and even in its failure and sorrow.
We would look always away from ourselves,
and behold the glory and the need of the world
that we may have the will and the strength to bring
the gift of gladness to others;
that with them we stand to bear
the burden and heat of the day
and offer Thee the praise of work well done.
Amen..

- Bishop Charles Lewis Slattery

Revive My Soul Again

There is a balm in Gilead
To make the wounded whole;
There is a balm in Gilead
To heal the sin-sick soul.

Some times I feel discouraged,
And think my work's in vain,
But then the Holy Spirit
Revives my soul again.

There is a balm in Gilead
To make the wounded whole;
There is a balm in Gilead
To heal the sin-sick soul.

If you can't preach like Peter,
If you can't pray like Paul,
Just tell the love of Jesus,
And say He died for all.

There is a balm in Gilead
To make the wounded whole;
There is a balm in Gilead
To heal the sin-sick soul.

- African American Spiritual

Amazing Grace

Amazing grace! How sweet the sound
That saved a wretch like me.
I once was lost, but now am found,
Was blind, but now I see.

'Twas grace that taught my heart to fear,
And grace my fears relieved.
How precious did that grace appear
The hour I first believed.

Through many dangers, toils and snares
I have already come;
'Tis grace hath brought me safe thus far
And grace will lead me home.

The Lord has promised good to me
His word my hope secures;
He will my shield and portion be,
As long as life endures.

Yea, when this flesh and heart shall fail,
and mortal life shall cease,
I shall possess within the veil,
A life of joy and peace.

When we've been there ten thousand years
Bright shining as the sun,
We've no less days to sing God's praise
Than when we've first begun.

- John Newton, 1760

The Infinite Goodness of God

I had a few days ago an insight which consoled me very much.
It was during my thanksgiving, when I make
a few reflections upon the goodness of God, and
how should one not think of this at such a time, of that
infinite goodness, uncreated goodness, the source of all goodness.

...

I saw written as in letters of gold this word, "Goodness"
which I repeated for a long time with indescribable sweetness.
I beheld it, I say, written upon all creatures, animate and
inanimate,
rational or not, all bore this name goodness. ...

I understood then that all these creatures have of goodness and
all the services and assistance that we receive from each of them
is a benefit which we owe to the goodness of God
who has communicated to them something of his infinite goodness
so that we may meet it in everything and everywhere.

- St. Thérèse Couderc, 1865

In Stillness, You Can Hear God

I speak to you.
Be still
Know I am God.

I spoke to you when you were born.
Be still
Know I am God.

I spoke to you at your first sight.
Be still
Know I am God.

I spoke to you at your first word.
Be still
Know I am God.

I spoke to you at your first thought.
Be still
Know I am God.

I spoke to you at your first love.
Be still
Know I am God.

I spoke to you at your first song.
Be still
Know I am God.

- *Essene Gospel of Peace*

Just Ask and I'll Be There

And heavier came each task;
'Why doesn't God help me?' I wondered.
He answered, 'You didn't ask.'

I wanted to see joy and beauty
But the day toiled on gray and bleak
I wondered why God didn't show me
He said, 'But you didn't seek',
I tried to come into God's presence;
I used all my keys in the lock.
God gently and lovingly chided,
'My child, you didn't knock.'
I woke up early this morning,
And paused before entering the day;
I had so much to accomplish
That I had to take time to pray.

- Author Unknown

The Comfort of Christ's Love

Blessed Jesus, in the comfort of your love, I lay before you the memories that haunt me, the anxieties that perplex me, the despair that frightens me, and my frustration at my inability to think clearly. Help me to discover your forgiveness in my memories and know your peace in my distress. Touch me, O Lord, and fill me with your light and your hope. Amen..

- Grace Cathedral, San Francisco

Prayer for the Assistance of Virgin Mary

O most beautiful flower of Mount Carmel,
Fruit of the Vine, splendorous of Heaven.
Blessed Mother of the Son of God,
Immaculate Virgin,
assist me in this my necessity.
O Star of the Sea, help me
and show herein you are my mother.
O Holy Mary, Mother of God, Queen of Heaven and earth,
I humbly beseech you from the bottom of my heart
to succor me in my necessity.
There are none that can withstand your power,
O, show me here you are my mother.
O Mary, conceived without sin,
pray for us who have recourse to Thee.
Sweet Mother, I place this cause in your hands.
Amen..

- Catholic Liturgy

Help Them Through Their Season of Loss

Father, I pray for (name one or more) and others in my circle of
family and friends who are grieving... They're hurting for many
reasons, and I ask You to help them through this season of loss.
I reach out to You, the Father of compassion and the Source of
every comfort, asking You to touch them with Your unfailing love
and kindness. Be their God who comforts them as they're going

through their struggles, and bring them through the tough things ahead. Come alongside them in their pain, and strengthen them so they'll one day be able to help others who face the same struggles.

- Wilber Baxter, 1957

Open Our Hearts to the Cries of the Suffering World

Let us see one another through eyes
enlightened by understanding and compassion.

Release us from judgment so we can receive the stories
of our sisters and brothers with respect and attention.

Open our hearts to the cries of a suffering world
and the healing melodies of peace and justice for all creation.

Empower us to be instruments of justice and equality everywhere.

- Author Unknown

Conclusion

Let's Be Grateful For Each Other and Be Grateful Together: Prayer Circles

In closing, we thought we would share with you one last way that you can express all of this newfound gratitude, and that is by opening up. The idea is simple. A blessing circle is a place for sharing stories, photos, videos, and prayers of gratitude with friends and loved ones. The more people you can get to align with you, the sooner you will discover the positive power of prayer and reap the many benefits that come from doing so. Now, we want to spread that gift and help you become cheerleaders for others who have tapped into the power of thankfulness by forming your own Power of Prayer Blessings Circle. We make it easy for you with our tips for starting a circle.

Opening to the Power of Prayer

1. As the organizer of the Circle, consider yourself the host or hostess, almost as if you have invited a group of friends—or people you hope will become friends—to your dinner table.

Your role is to help guide conversations and serve up a feast of interesting stories about gratitude or nuggets of information to share that will keep the conversations meaningful, inspiring, and ultimately bring to life the power of gratitude in all the lives of those gathered in your circle.

2. Create a Mission or Goals for your Circle.

What do you want to accomplish? How will you manifest this in your own life and the lives of those in your circle?

Will you share prayers, stories, inspiring quotes, guided meditations?

Create a plan for guiding your group through the practice of Prayer.

3. Decide Whether to Meet Online or In Person.

The exciting thing about the Internet is that you can create a

Circle and community online and connect friends and colleagues from across the country—and the world. See our

Facebook page for inspiration. Or you may want to create an in-person circle with friends in your neighborhood or town.

4. Send out evites and invites, and make phone calls to invite members to your Circle.

Ask everyone to invite a friend and spread the word about your new group.

5. Select a meet-up place.

Often guides will invite in-person communities to meet at their home. Or you may opt for a local coffee shop or another comfortable meeting place where you can gather regularly.

6. Create a calendar of meet-up dates and distribute to your group.

7. In this book, we have lots of prayers, inspirational quotes. And passages from the Bible to use as prompts for discussions.

Please feel free to tap into these resources.

Circles of Grace

These simple suggestions should help you and your Circle get started. Remember, nothing is cast in stone, and you can feel free to improvise until you find your comfort zone. We guarantee you will come away from these gatherings feeling inspired and challenged and with exciting new ideas to share.

First, begin by welcoming your guests. Go around the circle, with each person introducing themselves. For example, "I am Mary Smith and I live in Ohio. I am a writer, literacy volunteer, and mother of two."

Next read a passage of poetry, prayer, or prose. Now, go clockwise around the circle, and ask each participant why she or he is here and what spiritual sustenance he or she is seeking.

Ask a volunteer to read her favorite prayer or quote.

These group gatherings are wonderful, but personal sharing and discussion of goals can be intimidating at first, so be mindful of your group, and you'll sense when you will need to wrap things up. Always end on a high note by asking each person to share a prayer story and a blessing to appreciate with gratitude. May your transformation be your inspiration!

Index

Buddhist prayers and writings

Cancer

Change and Passages

Compassion

Courage

Dedication to God

Despair, Grief, and Sadness

Graces to Say – Blessings for Meals

Guidance

Health & Healing

Hope

Irish prayers & blessings

APR 0 6 2018

CPSIA information can be obtained
at www.ICGtesting.com
Printed in the USA
BVOW06s2253161217
502766BV00005B/6/P